WITH
ANTHONY TROLLOPE
IN NEW ZEALAND

WITH
ANTHONY TROLLOPE
IN NEW ZEALAND

Edited By
A. H. REED

Illustrations By
SID SCALES

A. H. & A. W. REED
Wellington :: Auckland :: Sydney :: Melbourne
FOR THE DUNEDIN PUBLIC LIBRARY.

First Published 1969

A. H. and A. W. Reed

182 Wakefield Street, Wellington
29 Dacre Street, Auckland
51 Whiting Street, Artamon, Sydney
357 Little Collins Street, Melbourne

© A. H. REED

TO
MARGARET AND JIM,
MALCOLM, ELIZABETH and LOUISE

First edition of 1,550 copies numbered and signed
of which this is

№ _488   *a H Reed*

The financial responsibility for this book has been undertaken by the Reed Publications Fund of the Dunedin Public Library.

The cost of illustrations has been met by a grant from the Otago Early Settlers Association's Reed Publications Fund.

SBN 589 00407 7

Printed in 11/13 Baskerville by
the Otago Daily Times Limited, Dunedin,
and bound by L. D. Hanratty Limited, Wellington.

PREFACE

ANTHONY TROLLOPE visited the South Pacific colonies in 1871 and 1872, and told the story of his travels in *Australia and New Zealand,* published in 1873 by Chapman and Hall. In the same year an Australian edition was published in Melbourne by George Robertson. In 1874 Chapman and Hall published *New Zealand* in a separate volume. The text of the present book is based upon the Melbourne edition.

The only alterations made in text and punctuation, are the breaking up of a few lengthy paragraphs. Footnotes, except where identified as Trollope's, are those of the present editor.

Mr and Mrs Trollope arrived at Bluff by the *Albion* on Saturday, August 3, 1872, and left Auckland by the San Francisco mail steamer *Nebrasca* on Thursday, October 3. At the period of their visit, Anthony was fifty-seven years of age.

This book is designed to tell, in Trollope's own words, the story of his travels in New Zealand: the places he visited, the people he met, and his personal views of the country and its people. It omits some historical and biographical material readily available elsewhere—such as New Zealand's early history. And so we accompany the novelist wherever he goes, sharing his varied experiences and seeing places and people through his spectacled eyes.

Anthony Trollope's name was first heard by me when, in 1895, at nineteen years of age, I was in Auckland, boarding with a lady who afterwards became my mother-in-law. "Belle," she said one morning to her daughter, "when you're down at the library, bring me one of Anthony Trollope's novels." I thought, what an unfortunate name. T. H. S. Escott, however, tells us that it was coined by William the Conqueror who, when one of his followers, during a hunting expedition, killed three wolves, dubbed him Troisloup.

In the 1890s, following the publication of his *Autobiography* in 1883, Anthony Trollope's star was still in declension, but rose again soon after the turn of the century. It was then, in Dunedin, that a well-read fruiterer, Walter Bull, brought him under my notice again. At that time, prior to World War I, unabridged classics, cloth-bound, in some cases illustrated, were published at one shilling net — New Zealand price 1s 3d. Though books were cheap, money was scarce. I bought a Trollope, added a book at a time, until eventually a set of most of his novels occupied a shelf. I still have them; most have been read several times, and my love for them has never waned.

To any who have not yet made the acquaintance of Trollope, and would risk coming under his spell, may I suggest the Barsetshire series, six titles in all, each complete in itself, beginning with *The Warden,* though perhaps it might be better to start with the next in the series, *Barchester Towers.*

And now, after nearly three-quarters of a century since I became acquainted with his name, I am prompted to reissue—published for the first time in New Zealand — Anthony Trollope's own story of his visit to this country.

Trollope tells us in an entertaining manner his impressions of persons and places. But what did the people of New Zealand have to say to and about him as he travelled among them? Here an attempt has been made to trace, in such contemporary newspaper and other sources as are available, the impression left upon the people of these islands a century ago by this great Victorian writer. These local chronicles have never previously been gathered together and, it is believed, will form an interesting and important footnote to Trollope's own story.

The book has been divided into four main parts—Otago, Canterbury, Wellington and Auckland, supplemented with contemporary press references and other material relating to the novelist. In some instances, notably in Captain Gilbert

Mair's *Reminiscences,* we are provided with interesting material not included in Trollope's own story.

I am greatly indebted to the editors of the several newspapers which provided glimpses of the " tireless traveller " as he passed through the country. How greatly is history dependent upon the newspapers which recorded for us the day-to-day happenings of the past. For various courtesies thanks are accorded to the Alexander Turnbull Library, the Director-General Department of Lands and Survey, the Brett Publishing Company, Miss Mary Ronnie, M.A., Misses Mercer, Comer and Randle, Miss M. M. Pryde, O.B.E., Miss M. Garden, Mr Arnold Wall, O.B.E., Mr D. W. Sinclair, Mr R. Duthie, B.A., Mr Euan Miller, M.A., Rev. J. T. Gunn, B.A., Professor R. G. Hargreaves, Mr R. A. Cant, Mr Allan Doig, Mr A. H. Harman, Mr R. Labone; and as in the case of all my books, Mr A. W. Reed, Chairman of Directors, A. H. & A. W. Reed.

A. H. REED.

153 Glenpark Avenue,
Dunedin.
August 30, 1969.

CONTENTS

ILLUSTRATIONS

MAPS

ANTHONY TROLLOPE

A FEW INTRODUCTORY NOTES

DICKENS, Thackeray and Trollope, in that order, are sometimes linked as the three greatest literary giants of the nineteenth century. Anthony Trollope, a Londoner, born on 24th April, 1815, was Dickens's junior by three years and Thackeray's by four. He was the son of a solicitor who is said to have some of the characteristics of Dickens's Wilkins Micawber, and who died in 1885, leaving his family in straitened circumstances.

Anthony received his earlier education at Harrow where, he tells us in his *Autobiography,* he had an unhappy time—a poor boy among the aristocrats. Later he spent three years at Winchester College. He came of a gifted family. His mother, Frances, and his brother, Thomas Adolphus, both became well-known Victorian novelists.

At nineteen years of age Trollope obtained a junior clerkship in the General Post Office, and in the employ of the Post Office he remained for thirty years. In 1841 he was transferred to Ireland as surveyor's clerk, and was later promoted to surveyor. In 1844 he married Rose Hesseltine, daughter of an English bank manager. Trollope's biographers tell us but little about Rose. Michael Sadleir, however, says that she and Anthony "lived in untroubled amity; . . . she helped him in the ordering of his work; entertained his friends; travelled in his company; and provided just that background of calm, well-managed comfort which was essential to so hard a worker." What better tribute could be paid to her?

Trollope's position in Ireland entailed much travelling to inspect post offices, and this enabled him to acquire useful background material for some of his novels. He spent several years in Ireland, and during that period made his first venture into authorship. In 1847, at 32 years of age, he wrote *The Macdermotts of Ballycloran;* this was followed in 1848 by *The*

Kellys and the O'Kellys; but neither of these brought him fame or fortune.

The famous Barchester series began with *The Warden,* in 1855, with a first edition of 1,000, 700 of which were sold, and the remainder relegated in later years to a cheap edition. This was followed in 1857 by *Barchester Towers,* for which, and *The Warden,* he received a total of from £700 to £800 during the next twenty years. Since his death, tens of thousands of these and the other Barchester novels have been published. In all, between 1847 and 1884, over sixty books were published, several of them, including the *Autobiography,* posthumously. During his lifetime his novels brought him a total of over £70,000.

Trollope had an unusually varied career. Most of his novels were written while in the service of the Post Office, from which he retired in 1868. It is to him that we owe one of the amenities of urban life — the familiar red letterbox seen at street corners in every New Zealand city. Besides novel-writing, at various periods either before or after his retirement from the Post Office, Trollope edited several periodicals, and travelled, either on postal business or for pleasure, to America, the West Indies, Egypt, South Africa, Australia and New Zealand — usually accompanied by his wife. In sport he was known on the hunting field as a fearless cross-country rider.

He was not only the "tireless traveller " but also the tireless worker. During his voyage from Auckland on the return to London he was working on *Australia and New Zealand,* a book of 691 pages. He reached London in December 1872; the book was published in the following February or March, and for his labours he pocketed £1,300.

Several letters written in or when approaching New Zealand have survived. One of these, housed in the Alexander Turnbull Library, Wellington, is included in *The Letters of Anthony Trollope* (Oxford Press, 1951) and is reproduced in this book. Another, housed in Trinity College Library, Melbourne, is headed, "Off the Bluff, 3 August, 1872." The letter is addressed to his friend G. W. Rusden (1819-1903), then Clerk of the Legislature, Melbourne, and Trollope asks a number of questions relating to Victoria. "My dear Rusden," he wrote, "I have been using my time on board, writing two short preparatory chapters respecting your colony." He concludes the letter: "One word to say how much unaffected pleasure I have had in making your friendship."

Another letter was written at Wellington, 27 August, to Arthur Locker, editor of the *Graphic,* offering the manuscript of *Phineas Redux,* which was later published as a serial in that periodical, and for which Trollope received £2,500.

A special interest attaches to Trollope's friendship with G. W. Rusden. It appears that, while the novelist was in Australia, Rusden published *The Discovery and Settlement of Port Phillip,* and dedicated it to Trollope, who based one of his chapters on the publication. He was so impressed by Rusden's acquirements that he urged him to write histories of Australia and New Zealand. This task Rusden undertook, and his *History of New Zealand* appeared in 1881 during a residence in England. Rusden may have regretted yielding to Trollope's persuasive powers, for the history resulted in a celebrated libel case, *Bryce v. Rusden.*

John Bryce (1833-1913), later Native Minister in the New Zealand Parliament, was a pioneer settler in Taranaki in the sixties, and a captain in the Yeoman Cavalry which defended the town of Wanganui against the dreaded Hauhaus during the later period of the Maori wars. In his book Rusden accused Bryce of having, during a sortie, cut down women and children, and an action for libel followed. The evidence completely cleared Bryce of the charge, and the jury awarded him £5,000 damages.

Some years after Trollope's death an absurd accusation of unseemly conduct while in New Zealand was made against him (see page 54). Many years later Trollope's character was still more ridiculously impugned. In 1942, a letter extracted

11

from an album, was offered at Sotheby's auction rooms, and described in the catalogue as "one of the most extraordinary letters ever offered for sale;" and, states a note in *The Letters of Anthony Trollope,* "provoked vigorous controversy in the press."

> " Waltham Cross,
> March 24, 1861

"My dearest Miss Dorothea Sankey,

"My affectionate and most devoted wife is as you are aware, still living — and I am proud to say her health is good. Nevertheless it is always well to take time by the forelock and be prepared for all events. Should anything happen to her, will you supply her place—as soon as the proper period of decent mourning is over.

" Till then, I am your devoted Servant,

ANTHONY TROLLOPE."

It is difficult to credit that such a letter could be taken seriously by anyone of ordinary intelligence who knew anything whatever of Anthony Trollope; and astonishing that it could give rise to "controversy." In course of time the story reached New Zealand, where the letter was published, with a suggestion that, at the time of writing, Trollope, then 45, was in "the dangerous age", and a reference to "the lad Cupid".

The letter was admitted to be undoubtedly genuine, and Michael Sadleir, Trollope's biographer, endeavoured unsuccessfully to obtain particulars as to whence it came and its past history. "One thing is certain," said Sadleir, "the letter was not written seriously, and reveals no hidden romance in Trollope's life." There can be little doubt that it was written in fun to a child, and it can be assumed that the facts were purposely concealed by the owner in order that the value of the letter might be enhanced.

As for Rose, though we know but little about her, we do know that the marriage was a happy one. Nine years after the publication of the Dorothea Sankey letter, *The Letters of Anthony Trollope* was published, and there, preserved by Rose's granddaughter, we can read several letters of Anthony to his

12

wife. An earlier one, written when Trollope was absent in Paris on business, concludes, "God bless you my own dearest love." In almost the last letter he wrote, posted from the provinces only a few weeks before his death, he addressed Rose as "Dearest Love," and concludes, "God bless you. Your own A.T." Rose was six years Anthony's junior, was sixty-one when Anthony died, and outlived him thirty-five years, dying in 1917 at the age of 96.

Once and again in his novels Trollope has a passing reference to New Zealand, but there was an occasion when he proposed to use the name as the title of a publication. In 1851, when thirty-six years of age, he had read Carlyle's political thunderings in *Latter Day Pamphlets,* and a few years later submitted to his publisher the manuscript of a work by which, as Sadleir puts it, he hoped "to put the world to rights." The work was to be entitled *The New Zealander* — a good title for the New Zealand novel that Trollope unfortunately omitted to write! Unfortunately, too, this book, publication of which was declined, had no reference either to Maori or Pakeha, except the title, which was prompted by a well-known passage in T. B. Macaulay's review of von Ranke's *History of the Popes.* Referring to the Roman Catholic Church, Macaulay wrote: And she may still exist in undiminished vigour when some traveller from New Zealand shall, in the midst of a vast solitude, take his stand on a broken arch of London Bridge and sketch the ruins of St. Paul's." This was written in 1840, after news of the signing of the Treaty of Waitangi had been received in England.

It had been Trollope's good intention to show how the world could be "set to rights" and thus avoid the fulfilment of Macaulay's surmise. We may be thankful, however, that the novelist failed to find a publisher for his *The New Zealander.* Instead, he gave us the English classic which still holds its own after a hundred years—*Barchester Towers.*

A. H. R.

ANTHONY TROLLOPE
at about the period of his New Zealand visit

OTAGO

I HAD LANDED at Melbourne on 27th July, 1871, and left that place for New Zealand on the 29th July, 1872, having spent a year and two days in seeing the Australian colonies.[1] From Melbourne we took the steamer for The Bluff [Bluff], the name given to the southern part of the Middle Island.

The Bluff, at which we landed, is the seaport of Southland, and hence there runs a railway to Invercargill—which was its capital when, as a separate province, it had a capital,—and twenty miles beyond it to a place called Winton. On landing I immediately asked to be shown some Maoris, but was told that they were very scarce in that part of the country. Indeed, I did not see one in the whole province, and it seemed as though I might as well have asked for a moa,—the great bird which used, in former days, to stalk in solitary grandeur about the island.

The place at which we landed had a quay, and a railway, a post office, and two inns;—but it had nothing else. The scenery was wild and pretty,—more like the western sea-coast of County Cork than any other that I have seen. The land was poor, and for some distance around apparently useless.[2]

---

1. Mr and Mrs Trollope had a special interest in visiting Australia, where their son Frederic was a sheep-farmer in western New South Wales. Anthony's grandfather had been the youngest of the four sons of a baronet, Sir Thomas Trollope. Frederic settled in Australia, where he and his wife Susannah raised a family of eight children. Against all expectations, a member of the Australian family inherited the baronetcy, and Sir Anthony Trollope, became a citizen of New South Wales.
2. Trollope was unfortunate in what he saw. There is much productive land in Southland.

15

There were hills on all sides, and mountains in the distance. It would be impossible to imagine any country more unlike Australia—a remark which I may as well make once for all, and which may be applied to everything in New Zealand. The two countries both produce wool, and are both auriferous. Squatters and miners are common to them. But in all outward features they are dissimilar,—as they are also in the manners of the people, and in the forms of their Government.

I found myself struck, for a moment, with the peculiarity of being in New Zealand. To Australia generally I had easily reconciled myself, as being a part of the British Empire. Of New South Wales and Van Diemen's Land I had heard so early in life as to have become quite used to them,—so that I did not think myself to be very far from home when I got there. But New Zealand had come up in my own days, and there still remained to me something of the feeling of awful distance with which at that time I regarded the young settlements at the Antipodes,—for New Zealand is of all inhabited lands, the most Antipodean to Greenwich. I remembered the first appearance in public of the grim jokes attributed to Sydney Smith, as to the cold curate, and the hope expressed that Bishop Selwyn might disagree with the cannibal who should eat him.

The colony still retained for me something of the mysterious vagueness with which it was enveloped in early days, so that when landing at The Bluff I thought that I had done something in the way of travelling. Melbourne had been no more than New York, hardly more than Glasgow, certainly not so much as Vienna. But if I could find myself in a Maori pah [pa], —then indeed the flavour of the dust of Pall Mall would for the time depart from me altogether. Most travellers have experienced the feeling,—have anticipated a certain strangeness which they have never quite achieved. But when I reached

Invercargill, the capital of Southland, I felt exactly as I might have felt on getting out of a railway in some small English town, and by the time I had reached the inn, and gone through the customary battle, as to bedrooms, a tub of cold water, and supper, all the feeling of mystery was gone. I began to enquire the price of tea and sugar, and the amounts of wages which the men were earning; but had no longer any appreciation of my Antipodean remoteness from the friends of my youth.

I can hardly explain how it is that Invercargill, and indeed all New Zealand towns, are more like England than are the towns of Australia,—but so it is. The everlasting gum forests do not belong to New Zealand, and the trees which are indigenous to the soil are brighter in hue than the dull-coloured foliage of the eucalyptus tribe. And "the bush" at any rate in the Southern—or so called Middle,[1]—Island is not sempiternal, as it is over so vast a proportion of Australia. At first it struck me that there was an absence of timber, and in some places I found that fuel was terribly expensive, in consequence of the distance over which wood had to be carried. Again no animal is now to be seen in New Zealand different from those which are familiar to us in England. There is, I believe, a rat in the country whose ancestors are said to have existed there previous to the coming of the English,—though some naturalists cast a doubt even upon the rat,—but there is no other four-footed animal that has not been imported and acclimatised. There are a few native birds, but those which are commonly seen are to the eye in no way different from English birds. The moas have left their skeletons, which are to be seen standing in the museum in Christchurch from 11 to 13 feet high,—but the last moa died some say more than 1,000 years ago, while others contend that they existed down

---

1. New Zealand's nomenclature long changed to North, South, and Stewart Islands.

to the coming of the Maoris, who were supposed to have eaten the last of them not more than 250 years since. . . .

In New Zealand everything is English. The scenery, the colour and general appearance of the waters, and the shape of the hills, are altogether un-Australian, and very like to that with which we are familiar in the west of Ireland and the highlands of Scotland. The mountains are brown and sharp and serrated, the rivers are bright and rapid, and the lakes are deep, and blue, and bosomed among the mountains. If a long-sleeping Briton could be awaked, and set down among the Southland hills, and told that he was travelling in Galway or Cork, or in the west of Ross, he might be easily deceived, though he knew the nature of those counties well,—but he would feel at once that he was being hoaxed if he were told in any part of Australia that he was travelling among Irish or British scenery.

We were unfortunate in the time of the year, having reached the coldest part of New Zealand in the depth of winter. Everybody had told me that it was so,—and complaint had been made to me of my conduct, as though I were doing New Zealand a manifest injustice in reaching her shores at a time of the year in which her roads were all mud, and her mountains all snow. By more than one New Zealander I was scolded roundly, and by those who did not scold me I was laughed to scorn. Did I imagine that because August was summer in England, therefore it was summer at the other side of the world; or did I think that I should find winter pleasant in Otago, because winter might be preferable to summer at the other side of the world; or did I think that I should find winter pleasant in Otago, because winter might be preferable to summer in Queensland? I endeavoured to explain that I had no alternative,—that I must see New Zealand in winter or not see it at all; but one always fails in attempting to make one's own little arrangements intelligible to others, and I found it better to submit. I had come at the wrong time;—was very sorry for it, but would now make the best of it. Perhaps the roads would not be so very bad. I was assured that they could not possibly be worse.

Nevertheless as I had come to see scenery, I determined to see it as far as my time and strength would allow. I had learned that Lake Wakatip was the great object to be reached, —Wakatipu is the proper name, but the abbreviated word is always used. From Invercargill I could certainly get to Wakatip, as the coach was running, and from Wakatip I might possibly get down to Dunedin,—but that was doubtful. If not, I must come back to Invercargill. I hate going back, and I made up my mind that if the mud and snow were no worse than British mud or British snow, we would make our way through.

We were accompanied by a gentleman from Invercargill[1], whose kindness I shall never forget, and whose fortitude in adversity carried us on. After staying two days at Invercargill, —which is a thriving little Scotch town without any special attractions, but which boasts a single cab, and a brewer who was very anxious that I should take a barrel of his beer home to England in order that the people there might know what New Zealand could do in the way of brewing, and who generously offered to give me the barrel of beer for that purpose,—we started on our journey by rail to Winton.

Although I know how utterly uninteresting to the general reader are the little trials of a traveller's life, I cannot refrain from explaining that we,—I and my wife were "we,"—were constrained to send the bulk of our luggage on to Dunedin by steamer, as it was impossible to carry overland more than one or two leather bags, and that it was long before we regained our boxes. As in Australia, so in New Zealand, locomotion is

---

1. Mr W. H. Pearson, Commissioner of Crown Lands, Invercargill, at the request of the Government.

effected chiefly by means of coastal steamers. The boat in
which we had come from Melbourne to The Bluff, would
pass in its usual course up the eastern coast, touching at Port
Chalmers, the port for Dunedin; at Lyttelton, the port for
Christchurch; at Wellington, the capital, which lies at the
extreme southern point of the Northern Island, through Cook's
Strait which divides the two islands, to Nelson, and down
the western coast of the Middle Island to Greymouth and
Hokitika, and from that place back to Melbourne. This is
done every fortnight, and in the alternate week another
steamer takes the reverse course, reaching Hokitika direct from
Melbourne, making its way round to The Bluff, and returning
thence to its home in Melbourne.

There are also smaller boats plying occasionally from port to
port,—and in this way the New Zealanders travel from one
province to another;—but with all the conveyances with which
I have had dealings, these New Zealand steamboats are the
most regularly irregular, and heart-breaking. If a would-be
traveller should be informed that steamboats would start from
a certain port to another, one on the 1st and another on the
15th of the month, his safest calculation would probably be
to make his arrangements for the 8th. Of course travelling by
sea cannot be made as certain as that by land,—and equally
of course boats which depend for their maintenance solely on
freight must be dependent on the incidents to which freight
is liable. I make no complaint;—not even on the score that
I never could be at any place at the same time with my
clothes. I used to be unhappy, but accepted my misfortune as
a part of the necessity of the position. But it is right to say
that travelling in New Zealand was uncomfortable. We could
not carry our portmanteaus overland, and therefore trusted
them to the steamers with copious addresses, with many
injunctions to persons who naturally were not quite so strongly
interested in the matter as we were ourselves. After a long

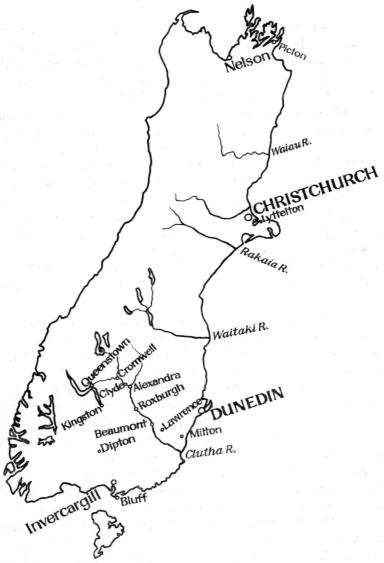

South Island of New Zealand showing places mentioned by Trollope.

and painful separation we and our luggage did come together again; but there was much of intermediate suffering. A hero, but nothing short of a hero, might perhaps sit down comfortably to dinner with the full-dressed aristocracy of a newly visited city, in a blue shirt and an old grey shooting jacket.

I will endeavour to say no more on a subject which at the time occupied too many of my thoughts. With great misgivings as to the weather, but with high hopes, we started from Invercargill for Lake Wakatip. Our first day's journey was by coach (after travelling to Winton by rail), which was tolerably successful, though fatiguing. A Swede drove us who owned the coach, and kept an inn half-way, at which we got a very good dinner. He was married to a half-caste Maori woman, and I made a note that the mixture of the breed on the female side seemed to be favourable to cookery. A better boiled turkey and plum-pudding were never put upon a table[1].

I did not like the Swede himself so well, as I entertained a suspicion that he made us pay double fare, as strangers to the country. I fancy that this practice is prevalent in Otago generally, which is a canny province, colonised by the Scotch, given to thrift, and prosperous accordingly. Indeed it was impossible not to remember the story of George III, who when charged a guinea by some innkeeper for a boiled egg, suggested with gentle sarcasm that eggs were probably scarce in that part of the country. " No, your Majesty;—but kings are." Travelling strangers are scarce in Otago, especially in winter,—and therefore it answers better to make something of the bird in the hand than to allure birds out of the bush by reasonable charges. For the present, perhaps, the practice may be prudent; but as the scenery of the country is both lovely and magnificent, as it has had bestowed upon it by nature all those attractions

---

1. See page 14, Appendix to Otago.

which make Switzerland the holiday playground of Europe, and as it is near enough to the growing cities of Australia to offer the same allurements to them, it may soon be well for the innkeepers up the country to consider whether it may not answer their purpose to establish some fixed rate of charges, and to look to what may be got from the public generally rather than to the individual victim of the moment. Again I make no complaint. It is better for the traveller to pay high prices for poor accommodation than to find none at all. In New Zealand the prices are no doubt very much higher that in Australia generally;—in Otago they are perhaps double the Australian prices; and in Australia they by no means startle the traveller by their lowness.

The first night we stayed at a squatter's house, and I soon learned that the battle between the squatter and the free-selector, of which I had heard so much in the Australian colonies, was being waged with the same internecine fury in New Zealand[1]. Indeed the New Zealand bitterness almost exceeded that of New South Wales,—though I did not hear the complaint so common in New South Wales that the free-selectors were all cattle-stealers.

The complaint made here was that the government, in dealing with the land, had continually favoured the free-selector at the expense of the squatter,—who having been the pioneer in taking up the land, deserved all good things from the country of his adoption. The squatter's claim is in the main correct. He has deserved good things,—and has generally got them. In all these colonies,—in New Zealand as well as New South Wales and Victoria,—the squatter is the aristocrat of

---

1. "When the Provincial Council met in December 1869, it at once plunged with avidity into a heated debate . . . the chief argument centred around the claims of the small mixed farmer and of the runholder." (The History of Otago, A. H. McLintock, 1949.)

the country. In wealth, position, and general influence he stands first. There are no doubt points as to which the squatters have been unjustly used,—matters as to which the legislature have endeavoured to clip their wings at the expense of real justice. But they have been too strong for the legislature, have driven coach and horses through colonial acts of parliament, have answered injustice by illegal proceeding, and have as a rule held their own, and perhaps something more. I soon found that in this respect the condition of New Zealand was very similar to that of the Australian colonies. The gentleman who accompanied us was the government land commissioner of the province, and, as regarded private life, was hand and glove with our host;—but the difference of their position gave me an opportunity of hearing the land question discussed as it regarded that province. I perceived that the New Zealand squatter regarded himself as a thrice-shorn lamb, but was looked upon by anti-squatters as a very wolf.

Lake Wakatip is about seventy miles from Invercargill, the road to it being fairly good,—for a "bush" road. The name must be taken in its colonial sense. There was hardly a tree to be seen throughout the journey, but the word has made its way over from Australia, and the traveller when he is out of the town is in the bush; and a country road which is merely formed and not metalled is a bush road though it pass across an open plain, or up a treeless valley. We passed up such a valley, with mountains on each side of us, some of which were snow-capped. We crossed various rivers,—or more probably the same river at various points. About noon on the second day we reached the lake at a place called Kingstown [Kingston], and found a steamer ready to carry us twenty-four miles up it to Queenstown, on the other side. Steamers ply regularly on the lake, summer and winter, and afford the only means of locomotion in the neighbourhood. But **no** sooner were we on board than the rain began to fall as it does only when the heavens are quite in earnest. And it was very, very cold. We could feel that the scenery around us was fine, that the sides of the lake were precipitous, and the mountain tops sharp and grand, and the water blue; but it soon became impossible to see anything. We huddled down into a little cabin, and endeavoured to console ourselves with the reflection that, though all its beauties were hidden from our sight, we were in truth steaming across the most beautiful of the New Zealand lakes. They who cannot find some consolation from their imagination for external sufferings had better stay at home. At any rate they had better not come to New Zealand in winter.

Queenstown is probably the biggest and most prosperous of the Otago gold-field towns. The greater portion of the province is divided into different gold-fields which are being worked with more or less success. The process at present is chiefly that of alluvial washing, which always goes before quartz-crushing. I had visited so many Australian goldfields that I determined not to devote myself to similar inspection in New Zealand;—and as I have written so much about Australian gold, I will say but little as to that of New Zealand. I found, however, that miners' wages in New Zealand were considerably higher than those in Australia, averaging as much as 10s a day for eight hours work, and running sometimes as high as £4 a week. I was assured that the miners, at any rate in Otago, do not themselves embark in speculation so constantly as do their brethren in Sandhurst and Ballarat. Surface gold-seeking, the work of washing the dirt extracted from gullies and river-beds, is of course carried out by the speculation of the seekers and washers themselves; and at this a man may earn nothing for three weeks, and 20s or £20 in the fourth week. In this work speculation is of course a necessity to the worker. But the men employed on deep sinking at weekly wages are not so commonly given to gambling as they are in

Australia. The opportunities for doing so are probably not so readily afforded to them. But if they do not gamble so much they drink more.

Queenstown on Lake Wakatip is a town of about 2,000 inhabitants,—looking, as is the case with all these towns, as though it were intended for double that number. It is built close down upon the water, and is surrounded by mountains, —on all of which the snow was lying. There are many towns so placed in Switzerland, and on the Italian lakes,—which in position this New Zealtnd mining borough much more closely resembles than anything at home; but the houses, and something in the fashion of the streets, the outside uses and bearings of the place declare it to be unmistakably English. The great drawback to New Zealand,—or I should more properly say to travelling in New Zealand,—comes from the feeling that after crossing the world and journeying over so many thousand miles, you have not at all succeeded in getting away from England. When you have arrived there you are, as it were, next door to your own house, and yet you have a two months' barrier between yourself and your home.

A steamer from Queenstown generally runs up to the top of the lake one day, returning the next, making the journey once or twice a week; but the good-natured captain, who, I believe, was also the owner of the boat, on being asked, at once consented to take us up and down in one day. The distance is about thirty-six miles, making the entire length of the lake about sixty miles. It was a bright clear cold day, with the temperature at freezing-point from morning to evening. There were two ladies in the party for whom cloaks and opossum rugs were very necessary. I myself spent a great part of the day within the genial influence of the funnel. But I enjoyed it greatly. I do not know that lake scenery can be finer than that of the upper ten miles of Wakatip;—although doubtless it can be very much prettier. The mountains for

the most part are bare and steep. Here and there only are
they wooded down to the water's edge,—and so much is
the timber in request for fuel and building, that what there
is of it close to the water will quickly disappear. As the
steamer gradually winds round into the upper reach, which
runs almost directly north and south, one set of peaks after
another comes into view. They are sharp and broken, making
the hill-tops look like a vast saw with irregular gaps in it.
Perhaps no shape of mountain-top is more picturesque than
this. The summits are nearly as high as those of Switzerland,
and that of Mount Earnshaw [Earnslaw] at the head of the
lake being 9,165 feet [West Peak 9,250ft. East Peak 9,165ft]
above sea level. The mountains themselves, however, do not
look to be so big as the Alps. There is no one peak which
strikes one as does the Matterhorn, no one head like the head
of Mont Blanc;—no one mountain which seems to be quite
so much of a mountain as the Yungfrau. But the effect of
the sun shining on the line of peaks was equal to anything
I had seen elsewhere.

The whole district around is, or rather will be in coming
days, a country known for its magnificent scenery. Among
the mountains there are vast glaciers;—but the means of
reaching them are not yet at the command of ordinary travellers.
To the south-west of Lake Wakatip, and nearer the coast, are
Lake Teanau [Te Anau] and the Manipori [Manapouri] Lake,
of the beauty of which I was told very much. The woods
come down to the water's edge, and in summer all is green
and sweet, secluded and soft. To the north-east is Wannika
[Wanaka] Lake, running into the province of Canterbury, in
sight of which stands Mount Cook, over 13,000 feet [12,349]
high. About forty miles to the north-west of Wakatip Martin's
Bay may be reached, on the western coast, at which place when
I was in Otago, a few settlers were struggling to make a

home[1]. I was assured that unless the government would do something for them,—would make them a road across to the lake, or send occasionally a ship to them with provisions, the place must be abandoned.

Down the coast, south from Martin's Bay, there is a series of so-called sounds, which are said to resemble closely the Norway Fiords. . . . I was there in the New Zealand winter, and could not reach the sounds on the coast or the lakes either to the north-east or south-west of Lake Wakatip.

From Queenstown we journeyed overland to Dunedin, the capital of Otago, and the journey was one which to me will ever be memorable. It is generally performed in three days. It took us six, during the first five of which we travelled in a buggy with a pair of tired horses. Our average daily distance was about twenty-five miles, our pace about three miles an hour, and the cost of travelling about 3s 6d a mile. When I think of the road which we traversed, I feel that the pace was good, and the price reasonable. But the tedium was great, and the inns at which we stopped were not delightful. The scenery, however, was grand almost throughout the journey. We came down the course first of one river and then another, crossing them now and again by means of double punts, which are fastened to ropes and carried over by the effect of the stream,—as is done on different bridgeless rivers in Italy. We journeyed on from one gold-field town to another, finding the people always in a state of prosperity. Ordinary labour throughout the country receives 5s or 6s a day,—or 4s, with rations. The little towns seemed to be well to do, all having banks and numerous hotels.

The life is rough; but is plenteous and comfortable. Things are ugly to European eyes, but are neither poor nor squalid.

---

1. The settlers incurred great hardships. The locality was found to be unsuitable for a settlement, and was long since abandoned.

There have been three successive styles of architecture in these towns, indicating different periods. The first is the canvas style, —in which men live in tents. That had passed away from the Otago gold-fields before our arrival. The second is the corrugated-iron period, beyond which as yet no advance has been made in many of the New Zealand towns. Corrugated iron does not make picturesque houses. It is very portable; very easily shaped; capable of quick construction; and it keeps out the rain. It is, however, subject to drawbacks. The rooms formed of it of course are small, and every word uttered in the house can be heard throughout it, as throughout a shed put up without divisions. And yet the owners and frequenters of these iron domiciles seem never to be aware of the fact. As I lay in bed in one of these metal inns on the road, I was constrained to hear the private conversation of my host and hostess who had retired for the night. "So this is Mr Anthony Trollope," said the host. The hostess assented, but I could gather clearly from her voice that she was thinking much more of her back hair than of her visitor. "Well," said the host, "he must be a — fool to come travelling in this country in such weather as this." Perhaps, after all, the host was aware of the peculiarity of his house, and thought it well that I should know his opinion. He could not have spoken any words with which at that moment I should have been more prone to agree.

On the fifth day, the worst of all, for the snow fell incessantly, the wretched horses could not drag us through the mud, so that I and the gentleman with me were forced to walk, and the twelve miles which we accomplished took us five hours,—we reached the town of Tuapika [Tuapeka] whence we were assured there would run a well-appointed coach to Dunedin. Tuapika is otherwise called Lawrence,— and it may be as well here to remark that in this part of New Zealand all towns have two names. The colonists give

one,—sometimes, as in the case of Tuapika, taking that of
the natives,—and the government gives another. We had come
through Dunedin [Dunstan] *alias* Clyde, through Teviot *alias*
Roxburgh, through Beaumont which had some other name
which I have forgotten, and at last reached Tuapika *alias*
Lawrence. The rivers and districts have been served in the
same way, and as the different names are used miscellaneously,
the difficulty which travellers always feel as to new localities
is considerably enhanced. At Tuapika we found an excellent
inn, and a very good dinner. In spite of the weather I went
round the town, and visited the Athenaeum or reading-room.
In all these towns there are libraries, and the books are strongly
bound and well thumbed. Carlyle, Macaulay, and Dickens
are certainly better known to small communities in New
Zealand than they are to similar congregations of men and
women at home. I should have liked Tuapika had it not
snowed so bitterly on me when I was there.

On the following day we got on board the well-appointed
coach at six in the morning. It certainly was a well-appointed
coach, and was driven by as good a coachman as ever sat
upon a box; but the first stage, which took us altogether six
hours, was not memorable for good fortune. There was a
lower new road and an upper old road. The former was
supposed to be impracticable because of the last night's snow,
and the man decided on taking the hills. As far as I could
see we were traversing a mountain-side without any track;
but there was a track, for on a sudden, as we turned a
corner, we found ourselves in a cutting, and we found also
that the cutting was blocked with snow. The coach could
not be turned, and the horses had plunged in so far that we
could with difficulty extricate them from the traces and pole-
straps. The driver, however, decided on going on. Shovels
were procured, and for two hours we all worked up to our
hips in snow, and did at last get the coach through the

So we went to work again with the shovels, and dug out first one animal
and then the other.

cutting. But it was not practicable to drive the horses down the hill we had ascended, and we therefore took them out and brought it down by hand—an operation which at any rate kept us warm.

We had hardly settled into our seats after this performance, before one of the leaders slipped into a miner's water-run, and pulled the other horse under the pole atop of him. The under horse was as it were, packed into the gully and buried, with his brother over him, like a tombstone. So we went to work again with the shovels, and dug out first one animal and then the other. We were wet through, and therefore a good deal the worse for our task, but the horses did not seem to mind it. At last we reached the town of Tokomairiro *alias* Milton, where comforts of all kinds awaited us. In the first place, there was a made road into Dunedin, and a well-horsed coach to take us. We had descended below the level on which the snows were lying. My wife found a kind hostess who took her to a fire and comforted her with dry stockings, and I got some dinner and brandy-and-water. About eight in the evening we reached Dunedin, alive, and in fair spirits,—but very tired, and more ready than ever to agree with that up-country innkeeper who had thought but little of the wisdom of one who had come travelling by winter in Otago.

. . . Otago is the most populous, and I believe I may add the richest province in New Zealand, and its capital, Dunedin, is its largest city. According to the census of 1871 the population of the province was 69,491, being something above a fourth of that of the whole colony. Dunedin contains about 21,000 people. The settlement of Dunedin was founded on 28th [23rd] March, 1848, when a small band of Scotch emigrants, under Captain Cargill, first landed, and pitched their tents on the present site of the town. The rise, both of the province and of the town, has been very quick, having been greatly accelerated by the rushes after gold made from the various

Australian colonies. It seems that from the first finding of gold in New Zealand, the gold-fields there have exceeded in popularity those of Australia. The higher rate of miners' wages would seem to justify this, were it not rather the result than the cause. I found that New Zealand still enjoyed much of the charm of novelty in reference to other pursuits as well as that of gold. The wool growers, graziers, agriculturists and miners of the younger colony were, I will not say, envied by Australians generally, but regarded as having had almost unfair advantages bestowed upon them. It is, however, an undoubted fact that during the past two years there has been a considerable re-emigration from the Australian colonies to New Zealand.

Dunedin is a remarkably handsome town,—and, when its age is considered, a town which may be said to be remarkable in every way. The main street has no look of newness about it. The houses are well built, and the public buildings, banks and churches are large, commodious and ornamental. It strikes a visitor as absurd that there should be six capitals in New Zealand, a country which forty years ago was cursed with cannibalism,—but it strikes him as forcibly with wonder that it should so quickly have possessed itself of many of the best fruits of civilisations. This prosperity has come, I think, less from any special wisdom on the part of those who endeavoured to establish New Zealand colonies on this or another scheme than from the fact that in New Zealand British energies have found a country excellently well adapted for their development.

In regard to Otago and Dunedin, it was the intention of the founders, or at any rate of those who instigated the founders, to establish an especially Presbyterian settlement. Doubtless many Scotch families did come out to it, and Scotch names are predominant. The Scotch have always been among the best,—or perhaps the very best,—colonisers that the world has produced. But Otago is by no means now an exclusively

Presbyterian province, nor is Dunedin an exclusively Presbyterian city. In the now united provinces of Otago and Southland the Presbyterians are less than half the population. As to Dunedin we have heard lately more of its desire to have a Church of England bishop of its own than of any other propensity. And it is going to have a bishop,—I may say has got one, though when I was there the prelate had not yet arrived[1].

A former bishop did indeed come out—but he was not approved of, and was returned, having never been installed. It is marvellous to me that the Australian and New Zealand sees can find English clergymen to go out to them. The pay is small,—generally not exceeding £500 a year. That bishops do not become bishops for money we are all prepared to admit. But the power also is very limited, the patronage almost none at all, and the snubbing to which they are subjected is excessive. It seemed to me that this latter process was exacerbated by the small remnant of baronial rank which is left to them. The colonial bishop is still called my lord;—and of course wears an apron—and lawn sleeves when he is in church. But there is a growing determination that the clergymen of one Church shall have no higher rank than those of another,—and that a Church of England bishop, therefore, shall have no special social position in his colony.

At present this feeling is less strong in New Zealand than in Australia, and is to a certain degree restrained by the quiet, unproclaimed action of colonial governors, who like these bishops and do what in them lies to preserve the rank. But the operation of the colonist's mind, even when he belongs to the Church of England, works in the other direction. I shall

---

1. Bishop Samuel T. Nevill, later Primate of New Zealand. His predecessor's practices were considered to be too high-church.

no doubt be told that bishops do not undertake their duties with any view to the places that may be assigned to them in walking out of rooms,—as to patronage, or even to power. But we know that authority cannot be maintained without its outward appendages, and that clerical authority has needed them quite as much as civil or military authority. . . . No house, or "palace," is provided. I was told that it was considered indispensable that the new bishop should be a member of Oxford or Cambridge, a gentleman distinguished for piety and eloquence,—and a man of fortune. "Upon my word I think you are very exigeant," I said to my informant. He answered me by assuring me that they had now got all that they asked. The colonial sees always do find bishops. There are six at present in New Zealand,—with a population about half as great as that of Manchester, of which not more than two-fifths belong to the Church of England.

The Provincial Council was not sitting, but I was shown the chamber in which it is held. The members sit, like Siamese twins, in great armchairs, which are joined together, two-and-two, like some semi-detached villas. I was specially struck by what I cannot but call the hyper-excellence of the room. There has been, in most of the New Zealand provinces, a determination that the Provincial Assembly shall be a real parliament, with a Speaker and Speaker's chair, reporters' galleries, strangers' galleries, a bar of the house, cross benches, library, smoking-room, and a " Bellamy,"—as the parliament refreshment-rooms are all called, in remembrance of the old days of the House of Commons at home. The architecture, furniture, and general apparel of these Houses,—such of them as I saw,—struck me as being almost grander than was necessary. The gentlemen as they sit are very much more comfortable than are the members in our own House at home, and are much better lodged than are the legislators in the States of the American Union. The Congress of Massachusetts sits in a building which has indeed an imposing exterior but the chamber itself inspires less awe than does that of Otago.

In one respect the New Zealand legislatures have preferred American customs to those which they left at home. They are paid for the performance of their legislative work. The pay of a member of the Provincial Council in Otago used to be £1 a day. It is now 19s 11½d. When this information was first given to me, I own that I disbelieved my informant, attributing to him an intention to hoax a stranger. But I was assured that it is so. And it was arranged in this way. The legislature bent on economy, reduced the salaries of various provincial officers, and with the high-mindedness for which all legislative chambers in free countries should be conspicuous, reduced their own allowances from 20s to 12s a day. But, on trial, it was found that the work could not be done for the money. The Otago gentlemen who came from a distance, could not exist in Dunedin on 12s a day,—which, if it be considered that a member of parliament should be paid at all, is surely very low in a country in which a journeyman carpenter gets as much. A proposition, however, to raise the sum again to 20s was lost by a small majority. The rules of the House did not permit the same proposition to be again brought before it in the same session, and therefore in another notice the nearest sum to it was named—and carried. The moderation of the members was shown in the fact, that a fraction under, and not a fraction over, the original stipend, was at last found to satisfy the feeling of the House. I think that in Otago a more general respect would be felt for its legislature if the gentlemen sitting in it altogether repudiated the receipt of the small sum, perhaps £50 per annum, which is paid for their services.

The chief products of Otago are gold and wool;—but agricultural pursuits are extending themselves in all parts of the province. The number of free-selectors, or "cockatoos," is increasing, and by their increase declare their own prosperity. Individually, they almost all complain of their lot,—saying that the growth of their corn is precarious, and its sale when grown effected at so poor a price as not to pay for the labour of producing it. The farmers are in debt to the banks, and their lands are not unfrequently sold under mortgage. But such complaints are general all the world over. No man is contented unless he can make a fortune,—and no man is contented when he has made a fortune. The squatters, the miners, the cockatoo farmers, and the labourers working for him, all say the same thing. They regret that they ever left England. It is a mistake to suppose that the colony is a blessed place. Argyleshire, or even County Galway is much better than Otago. But in Otago all men live plenteously. Want is not known. If a man fails as a free-selector, he still lives plenteously as a labourer.

I will quote a few words from a printed dispatch respecting Otago, sent home by Sir George Bowen, the Governor of the colony, in 1871—"after the lapse of only twenty-three years" —from the first settlement of the province,—"I find from official statistics that the population of the province of Otago approaches nearly to 70,000, that the public revenue, ordinary and territorial, actually raised thereon exceeds £520,000; that the number of acres farmed is above a million; that the number of horses exceeds 20,000; of horned cattle 110,000; and of sheep 4,000,000. The progress achieved in all the other elements of material prosperity is equally remarkable; while the Provincial Council has made noble provision for primary, secondary and industrial schools; for hospitals and benevolent asylums; for athenaeums and schools of art; and for the new university which is to be opened in Dunedin in next year."[1] I found this

---

1. The University of Otago Ordinance was passed by the Otago Provincial Council on June 3, 1869. Classes were first held in July 1871.

to be all true. The schools, hospitals and reading-rooms, and university, were all there, and all in useful operation;—so that life in the province may be said to be a happy life, and one in which men and women may and do have food to eat, and clothes to wear, books to read, and education to enable them to read the books.

The province is now—(1873)—twenty-four years old. . . . Poor Western Australia is forty-five years old, and, with a territory so large, that an Otago could be taken from one of its corners without being missed, it has only 25,000 inhabitants, and less than one million sheep,—sheep being more decidedly the staple of Western Australia than of Otago. I do not know that British colonists have ever succeeded more quickly or more thoroughly than they have in Otago. They have had a good climate, good soil, and mineral wealth; and they have not had convicts, nor has the land been wasted by great grants. In founding Western Australia but little attention was paid either to climate or soil,—land was given away in huge quantities, and convicts were introduced to remedy the evils, and to supply the want of labour which that system of granting lands produced. And in Western Australia gold has not been found. I know no two offshoots from Great Britain which show a greater contrast.

Otago possessed no railways in 1872,[1]—but a whole system of railways was in preparation,—partly as yet only on paper, and partly in the hands of working contractors. The system, indeed, is one intended to pass through the entire middle island, and to be carried out in conjunction with an equally extended system in the northern island. For, where public works are concerned, millions are spoken of in New Zealand with a reckless audacity that staggers an economical Englishman.

---

1. A railroad connected Invercargill with Bluff in the 1860's, and the Dunedin-Port Chalmers railway was opened in 1872.

Debt does not frighten a New Zealand Chancellor of the Exchequer. Legislators in New Zealand take a pride in asserting that every New Zealander bears on his own shoulders a greater debt than do any other people in the world. Telegraphic wires run everywhere in Otago, and before long railways in the low countries will be almost as common. As it was we determined to travel by coach into the next province of Canterbury—finding that the boats were uncertain, and that the coach ran three times a week from Dunedin to Christchurch. The coach takes three days, travelling about sixty miles a day, and stopping during the night. We were told that the journey was harassing and tedious, but it would not be so harassing and tedious as that we had already made;—and then, by this route, we should see the country.

Leaving Dunedin we rose up a long wooded hill, with a view to the right over the land-locked arm of the sea down to Port Chalmers, which is the port for Dunedin. It was a most lovely drive. The scenery of the whole country round Dunedin is beautiful, and this is the most beautiful scene of it all. After a drive of about sixteen miles we breakfasted at a place called Waikonaiti [Waikouaiti], at which we found the landlord firing guns up the chimney to put out the fire. In spite of this little confusion we were excellently provided,—getting a much better coach breakfast than used to be common in England.

I may now say a few words on the disagreeable nature of New Zealand names. Wai is the most common prefix to the names of places, and signifies water. When divided in this manner, from what follows, it would seem to form a very simple addition;—but in truth it makes the word complex, difficult to catch, and almost impossible to be remembered. There are no less than twenty-eight post towns beginning with Wai, and of course the post towns are but few in comparison with the less important places. In the North Island Nga, or

Ngate, is the prefex which the reader most frequently meets in records of the early days of New Zealand. It signifies son, and corresponds with the Scotch Mac and the Irish O.

. . . From Waikonaiti the coach goes on to Palmerston—which sounds more familiarly to English ears. As far as this place, a distance of about thirty-five miles, the road is as good as any in England;—but then there comes a change, and thence on into the bounds of the province the road was very bad indeed. The first night's rest was, for the coach, at a small town called Oamaru, and for us at a squatter's house four miles further on. This we reached at 9 p.m., and left the next morning at 6 a.m.;—hours at which in fully civilised countries one does not expect a stranger to entertain one; but we found our hostess expecting us at dinner, and in the morning she got up and gave us our breakfast. Twelve miles of as miserable a road as ever I travelled brought us to the Waitaki river, which is the boundary of the province.

It was a piercingly cold morning, and we felt aggrieved greatly when we found that we had to leave the coach and get into a boat. But the dimensions of our own hardships lessened themselves to our imagination when we found that two of the boatmen descended into the river, and pushed the boat for half a mile up the stream. During a part of the way three men were in the water, and yet the boat hardly seemed to move. For this service we were charged 2s apiece which sum was not included in the coach fare. Pitying the men because of their sufferings, I gave them something over "to drink." It was taken, but taken without thanks, and with evident displeasure, and handed over with the ferry money to the employer. In New Zealand, and in some lesser degree in Australia, you may ask any man, or any number of men to drink, without the slightest risk of displeasing them; but the offer of money is considered to be offensive. The drinking must be done at the bar of a public house; and the money must be paid to the publican and not to your friend who drinks. . . . The practice of shouting or "standing drinks all round," I found to be in full force in New Zealand. Even servants will refuse money offered to them. A poor girl whom I had injured, knocking down into the mud the line on which all her clothes were drying, though she was in tears at the nuisance of having to wash them again, refused the money that I offered her, saying that though she was only a poor Irish girl without a friend in the world, she was not so mean as that. Another girl told my wife, in perfectly friendly confidence, that she did not think she ought to take money. It is odd that so excellent a lesson should be learned so quickly. The pity is that in the course of years it will doubtless be unlearned.

There are many such rivers as the Waitaki running into the sea on the eastern coast of New Zealand, very dangerous in crossing, and the cause of many accidents. We were then in the depth of winter, and they are not then full. It is after the winter rains, and after the snows, when the mountains give up their load of waters, that the streams become full, and the banks overflow. In the spring the coaches often cannot pass, and are occasionally washed away bodily when the attempt is made. At other rivers besides the Waitaki there is a custodian, who is in some degree responsible for the safety of travellers, and who seems always to charge 2s a head, whether he preside over a ferry, with boat, and boatmen, or simply over a ford, across which he rides on horseback showing the way.

When across the Waitaki we found ourselves in the great Church of England province of Canterbury.

Anthony Trollope
as Otago Saw Him

A VINDICATION

A TELEGRAM published in the *Otago Daily Times* of August 5, 1872, reads: "Bluff, August 3. The *Albion* has arrived with the English mail. . . . Passengers for Dunedin . . . Mr and Mrs Trollope . . ."

On January 23, 1937, the same newspaper published an article by C. R. Allen, entitled "A Word for Anthony Trollope." This set me wondering whether, after a lapse of 65 years, it was possible that someone might still have first-hand memories of the great man. An enquiry in the newspaper elicited a very interesting response from Miss Edith Hodgkinson, daughter of a well-known citizen of Invercargill in the 1870's. Dr Samuel Hodgkinson, who had arrived at Nelson in 1842 as surgeon on the *Bombay*, and eventually settled in Southland. He was a member of the Southland Provincial Council, and later M.P. for Riverton. It was he who took steps to have the grave of Edward Gibbon Wakefield cared for in Wellington. Hodgkinson died in 1914, a few months before the outbreak of World War I. Miss Hodgkinson wrote:

"Sir,—I fully expected that several letters would appear in response to that by Mr A. H. Reed, asking for reminiscences of that very pleasant novelist of mid-Victorian England. . . . I was twelve years old when Anthony Trollope visited Invercargill, and his charm had already won me, for at ten I had read *Framley Parsonage* and part of *The Small House at Allington* in the Cornhill. . . . There were no lending libraries so far south in those days. The Invercargill Athenaeum, with its statue of Minerva, about which I remember much debate, came in the mid-seventies. It was in the little wooden Anglican church which occupied the same site as the present one, that I had, at a Sunday morning service, my sole vision of the famous author. He was the guest, if I mistake not, of the Rev. Pybus Tanner, first Anglican minister of Invercargill, a man as saintly as Trollope's Mr Crawley, and I should say, far easier to live with.

"A strange contrast—the clergyman, and the chronicler of clergymen—the one of barely medium height . . . with acquiline nose and large, wistful eyes, more soul than body; and the stalwart man of letters, whose tread shook the church, as he marched down the aisle to take his seat near the pulpit. In Mr Allen's article Trollope disclaims being either an Antinous or a six-footer. Well, if he was not actually six feet in height, he succeeded in looking much more. A burly, upstanding man with a massive head, made more leonine by the whiskers and beard of old Victorian days; these, with his hair greying, an English complexion as of one living much in the open, and kindly blue-grey eyes to match. Such was Anthony Trollope as I saw him those brief moments. And I can imagine his voice, hearty and genial, to match his aspect."

These reminiscences of Edith Hodgkinson have a special interest as an eye-witness description of the novelist the day following his arrival in New Zealand.

E. M. Lovell-Smith, in *Old Coaching Days* (Lovell-Smith and Venner, Christchurch, 1931), supplements Trollope's account of the Winton-Kingston coach journey: "The mail service between Riverton and Invercargill, prior to Cobb and Co's. arrival, was carried on foot by a Russian Finn, William Flint." In 1869 Flint acquired the coach service between Invercargill and Frankton. Lovell-Smith continues:

"A People's Line of coaches came on the road in 1871, and Flint found himself faced with opposition. He cut his fares, and arranged for the steamer *Antrim* to convey his passengers to Queenstown. His coach left Winton on the arrival of the train every Monday, stopped the night at Dipton, and reached Kingston next day at 6 p.m. . . . Mrs Flint, a comely Maori dame, and clever in the culinary art, kept a good table, as Anthony Trollope discovered. . . . In after years, speaking to the writer, Trollope's hostess said that she remembered the occasion of the famous novelist's journey through Dipton. 'The coach horses were very wild that morning; the leaders jumped out of their harness'."

Queenstown's *Wakatip Mail* provides us with the next information about Trollope, in its issue for Wednesday, August 7:

"Mr Anthony Trollope, who is making a tour of the Australian colonies, arrived in Queenstown last evening via Invercargill and Kingston, accompanied by Mr Pearson, Commissioner of Crown Lands. Today, the visitors and Mr R. Beetham, R.M., took a trip up the Lake in the *Jane Williams,* steamer. Such a distinguished tourist as Mr Trollope must be looked upon as a good authority, and we shall anxiously look forward for his opinion of the residents and the scenery of this land of lakes and mountains."

From this it appears that the Trollopes left Invercargill on the morning of Monday, August 5, a couple of days after their arrival. A paragraph in the *Cromwell Argus* of August 11, indicates that the visitors had only one complete day at Lake Wakatipu:

"Mr Anthony Trollope arrived here from Queenstown on his way to Dunedin, last Thursday evening, and left for Clyde the following day. Mr Trollope's literary abilities are thus noticed in Chambers's Encyclopaedia." . . .

The Lawrence "own correspondent" of the *Bruce Herald* wrote on Wednesday, August 14:

"The world-renowned and famous Anthony Trollope is expected in Lawrence from up-country, and I presume we may in very truth endorse the words of the poet:

'There's a chield amongst you takin' notes
An faith he'll print them.' [sic]

We shall as a matter of course be on our best behaviour, and receive him I hope as he ought to be received.   4 o'clock. Anthony Trollope has arrived, and I am told he is a tall, gruff-looking fellow. I have not seen him."

The Lawrence newspaper, the *Tuapeka Times*, of the 15th had this to say:

"Mr Anthony Trollope, with Mrs Trollope, and Mr W. H. Pearson, arrived at Lawrence shortly after one o'clock p.m. on Monday last. They had an exceedingly rough passage between Roxburgh and Tuapeka. They started from the former place at seven on the Sunday morning, but owing to the snow-storm were unable to travel further than to Beaumont, from which place they resumed their journey at eight o'clock the following morning, arriving as previously stated. The party proceeded to Dunedin by Cobb and Co's. coach on Tuesday morning. Mr Trollope will be able to give a graphic description of the goldfields of Otago, seeing that he travelled from Queenstown to Lawrence, including one full day's detention on account of the snow-storm, in five days. The distance between the two places is about 140 miles, and the roads are, to say the best of them, exceedingly bad. Mr Pearson must have been able to furnish Mr Trollope with valuable information regarding the goldfields, as he has never before visited them. However, the fact that he has existed in that lively village of Invercargill without losing the possession of his faculties, renders him peculiarly fitted to pilot a stranger through any country under the sun. Mr Trollope, we believe, while in Lawrence visited the Athenaeum, and of course was highly gratified to learn that the inhabitants of this fair corner of the earth read sometimes. . . . It was proposed to entertain Mr Trollope at a dinner in the Commercial Hotel, but owing to the uncertainty which prevailed as to the time of his arrival it did not take place."

Prior to this period Invercargill had been, for several years, the capital of the Southland Province which, against the wishes of Otago, had seceded, and in 1861 had been proclaimed a Province. It ran into financial difficulties, and in 1870, says Dr McLintock in *The History of Otago,* "ended its brief, and somewhat unhappy, existence." This may account for the somewhat flippant reference to Mr W. H. Pearson.

Pearson and the Trollopes had travelled from Queenstown for the first five days by buggy, with the purpose, probably, of seeing the country more leisurely than by coach.

The following letter appeared in the *Tuapeka Times*:

"Sir,—Can you tell me the reason why there was such a rush to the Athenaeum last week? Amongst those most frequently at the institution recently I noticed several who set themselves up as great authorities in literature, and who are in the habit of claiming familiarity with the writings of every author that wrote since the expulsion of Adam from the garden of Eden. Is the explanation suggested by a friend of mine, viz., that many who intended to be present at the dinner proposed to be given to Mr Trollope, wanted to find out the titles of the books that gentleman has written, in order that they might not be considered ignorant cusses, correct? Yours truly, IGNORAMUS."

The editor's non-committal reply was, " We don't know."

It will be recalled that snow fell incessantly during the journey between Beaumont and Lawrence, and that Pearson and Trollope had to walk the whole distance, twelve miles; "the wretched horses," said Trollope, "could not drag us through the mud." On the 14th the Dunedin *Evening Star* published the following telegram from Queenstown: " The most severe weather ever felt by the oldest inhabitant is ruling. Business, mining, and almost everything is at a standstill in consequence." This was the snowstorm through which the Trollopes travelled from Lawrence to Milton. Referring to another part of the Queenstown-Dunedin route, Lovell-Smith wrote:

"The cold was most intense, the snow freezing as it fell, and so thick that one could scarcely see a yard in front of one. Kemp's was reached at 10.30, and Craig was so benumbed that he had to be lifted off the box. His beard was one solid mass of ice, gloves as hard as boards, and comforter and other clothing frozen."

The same writer adds something to Trollope's graphic account of the August 14 journey from Lawrence to Milton in the coach driven by Tommy Pope. Lovell-Smith writes:

"Leaving Lawrence in the coach, the travellers arrived at a cutting at Waitahuna to find the road blocked with snow. Pulling up his team, Pope procured some shovels from Edie's farm nearby and set to work to clear away the snow. Working away with a will, Anthony Trollope remarked that he was 'more at ease with a pen than a shovel'. After the snow had been cut to a depth of a foot or so, the driver led a coach-horse back and forth over it until it was trampled down enough to allow the coach to proceed. Further along the road Pope found the snow to be so deep that it would take a month to melt away, so he decided to take the coach over the crest of the hill. Upon reaching the top, the horses were taken out of the coach and placed in charge of the other male passenger. Then Pope and Trollope proceeded to pull the coach down-hill by hand; not that it needed much pulling, and guided it safely to the bottom of the hill. Mrs Trollope wore a crinoline, and as she walked down the hillside, her petticoats underneath became balled up with the soft snow. 'She was an enormous size, and a wonderful sight to behold,' remarked Pope in later years, when referring to the novelist's trip with his wife."

E. M. Lovell-Smith died in 1950 at the age of 74 and, says an obituary notice in the *Otago Daily Times,* "devoted many years of patient research" in collecting material for his book. It may be assumed that this independent story of the Lawrence-Milton coach drive was obtained first-hand from Tommy Pope —"as good a coachman as ever sat upon a box," says Trollope.

Robert Gilkison, in *Early Days in Central Otago* (Dunedin. Otago Daily Times, 1930 [first edn.], Whitcombe and Tombs, 1936), referring to Trollope's journey through Otago, wrote:

"He had accomplished a journey few visitors, if any, had ever attempted." It was "impossible to find, in this freshly-opened country, the amenities or comforts of the inns of the Old Land. And so many travellers found, as Anthony Trollope also discovered, that the little hotels at which they had to stay were the serious drawback to a long coaching journey. Most of these had been hastily erected in the days of the first rushes to accommodate the largest number of people in the smallest possible space."

Recalling what had happened during the arduous Queenstown-Dunedin journey, especially during the last two days, it can well be imagined that the Trollopes arrived at Dunedin after a fourteen-hour journey at eight o'clock on the night of the 14th, almost at the point of exhaustion. The news that they were travelling by way of Queenstown and Central Otago would have already reached Dunedin. Whether they were given a civic courtesy-call at the hotel we do not know, but it is evident by inference that Trollope was interviewed that evening by the *Otago Daily Times*.

On the morning of the 15th the *Otago Daily Times* announced in a "local."

". . . a conversazione . . . will be held this evening. . . . The musical part of the entertainment is in the charge of Mr A. J. Towsey. . . . We are glad to be able to announce that Mr Anthony Trollope arrived in town yesterday afternoon and will take part in the proceedings of the evening. Everyone will be glad to make the acquaintance of an author of such world-wide fame as Mr Trollope."

Up to that point nothing save the weather seems to have marred the serenity of the journey. Trollope did not attend the conversazione and this caused a change of attitude towards him. The press of Otago, which showed him scant courtesy, were probably unaware of the cause of his absence.

The conversazione (gentlemen 3/- and ladies 2/-) was held on the 15th, in celebration of the anniversary of the birth of Sir Walter Scott. Its purpose was the foundation of a University Sir Walter Scott scholarship. On several days previously an advertisement in the *Otago Daily Times* had announced that Professors Black and McGregor would deliver addresses, and it is obvious that Trollope was unaware, until after his arrival the previous night, that his presence was expected.

The *Bruce Herald's* "own correspondent" wrote, apparently on the morning of the 16th, when the Trollopes were already on their way to Christchurch:

"Anthony Trollope is here, but has given no sign. He was expected at the conversazione, but did not put in an appearance. It is said that he sent someone to see if it was a very fashionable affair, and if it was, he would go, but the report not being sufficiently satisfactory, he stayed away, when from all I hear Mr Anthony Trollope is not likely to increase the number of his colonial readers by the geniality of his nature or the kindly reminiscences of his visit he will leave in the minds of those who have come in contact with him."

From Anthony himself we learn nothing of all this, and he was probably quite unaware that he had unintentionally stirred up a hornet's nest, the cause of which seems fairly evident. Trollope tells us that before leaving Invercargill, arrangements had been made for their luggage to be sent on by coastal steamer, with the expectation that it would be awaiting them at Dunedin, and it would not have been until the morning following his arrival that he would have found to his dismay that it had not arrived. If there was any truth in the report sent to the *Bruce Herald,* it would have been for the very reason that it was a " fashionable gathering " that he absented himself from the conversazione. It was probably this function that he had in mind when referring to his errant luggage: "A hero, but nothing short of a hero, might perhaps sit down comfortably to a dinner with the full-dressed aristocracy of a newly visited city, in a blue shirt and an old grey shooting jacket." And even those must have been the worse for wear after the strenuous journey through mud and snow.

Brusque and bluff he was; gruff he could be; but not a snob; not Anthony Trollope. Captain Gilbert Mair who, a little later, accompanied him to the Hot Lakes region, said of him: "He hated snobs and society snobbishness with a deadly hatred." T. H. Escott, who knew him well, and who wrote his biography in 1913, refers to him as " among the broadest-minded, kindest-hearted of men." Lack of decent clothing may not, however, have been the only reason for his absence at the gathering. After the gruelling Central Otago journey the Trollopes must have had a very busy day before leaving for Christchurch on the following morning. A further reason may be suggested by a report of the gathering sent to the *Bruce Herald* by its Dunedin correspondent: "It appears to me that the management was a great bungle, having evidently been placed in the hand of a man who didn't understand the workings."

A previously unpublished incident in Trollope's busy life may appropriately illustrate his readiness to respond to requests to speak at public gatherings. In the Dunedin Public Library's Henry and Jennie Johnston collection of autograph letters, Henry Johnston, then secretary of the Glasgow Athenaeum, records a meeting with the novelist:

"I met Anthony Trollope by appointment at the Athenaeum Club, Pall Mall, on 15th July, 1869. I had a white card and a free hand to engage as many eminent lecturers for the following winter course at the Glasgow Athenaeum as I could secure, but was seriously handicapped by the extremely limited amount of money placed at my disposal for that purpose. It was therefore with some trepidation that I kept my appointment with such a popular and successful litterateur as Anthony

Trollope. On entering the Club I found waiting for me a tall, breezy, sun-tanned, farmer-like man with a hearty manner and an encouraging handshake. I had carefully intimated beforehand the object of my visit. He had evidently thought the matter well over, and after some enquiry regarding the Institution, he frankly acceded to my request. I was of course much gratified, but the delicate part of the negotiations had yet to come—his terms. This question I approached delicately without betraying the poverty of the Institution I represented, but he waved the matter brusquely aside. 'Do not speak of terms,' he said; 'when a man has something to say, and a suitable place and opportunity are offered him for saying it, that should be sufficient for him.' I thanked him and said he would at least allow us to pay his travelling expenses. 'I'll come,' he said at last, 'but say no more about money.' What he had to say was about 'Prose Fiction as a Rational Amusement.' The lecture was one of the most successful of a brilliant course."

From the Dunedin press we learn nothing of Trollope's movements on the 15th. The sole references relate to his absence from the conversazione. The following advertisement appeared in the *Otago Daily Times* on the 15th:

ANTHONY TROLLOPE'S NOVELS

may be had at

WISE'S LIBRARY

Subscription 21/-

New books and magazines by every Suez mail.

In a report of the conversazione it was stated in the *Otago Witness* of the 24th August, that:

"His Honour Mr Justice Chapman presided, and there was a crowded attendance, both of ladies and gentlemen. Addresses were delivered by the chairman and by Professors Black and McGregor. It had also been expected that Mr Anthony Trollope

would take part in the proceedings, but those present were
doomed to disappointment, for that gentlemen did not attend.
The committee, however, appear to have provided against the
contingency of Mr Trollope's non-appearance, for Professor
McGregor stated, in his introductory remarks, that a short
time before the proceedings commenced, he received a letter
from the committee couched in the following terms: 'If Mr
Anthony Trollope comes to make a speech, we will hold you
excused. If he does not, you must make a speech; and if
you don't make a speech, we will advertise you as the cause
of the ruin of the affair.' It is only justice to Mr McGregor to
say that his very able speech, which secured for him the close
attention of the audience, amply compensated for the absence
of Mr Trollope."

In the same issue of the *Otago Witness,* "Sigma," (perhaps
the forerunner of "Civis" of later years), had this to say in
"Passing Notes":

"Presumably, at least, the conversazione, in celebration of
Sir Walter Scott's birthday, may be considered a success, though
those who were present at it, say that the proceedings were
rather tame. The non-appearance of Mr Anthony Trollope,
and unwillingness of the audience to promenade, deprived the
affair of two of its principal features. Still, the speeches of
Judge Chapman and Professor McGregor, were worth going
to hear and formed a pleasant break to the intellectual torpor
that has prevailed in Dunedin for some time past."

On September 5, three weeks after Mr Trollope had left
Dunedin, the *Tuapeka Times* found further grounds for
disparagement:

"We have been informed, on what we consider reliable
authority, that the expenses of Mr Anthony Trollope, while in
Otago, were paid by the Provincial Government. We presume
the Provincial authorities by this means sought to ensure the
good opinion of Mr Trollope and, as equivalent for the sum
expended, to give a glowing description of the Province,
published in some British newspaper or magazine. Considering
the circumstances, and the way Mr Trollope rushed through
Otago, we do not think their object likely to be accomplished.

At any rate Mr Trollope cannot be in a position to write more accurately of Otago than he did of Queensland. Ordinary people cannot see what claim Mr Trollope has, to have his expenses paid by the countries he visits. If he contracts to write upon them, of course it is a different matter."

This derogatory report, however, was not allowed to go uncorrected. . . . "It having been reported," stated the *Otago Witness* on September 21, "that the Provincial Government defrayed Mr Anthony Trollope's expenses during his recent tour through the Province, we are requested to deny the truth of the rumour. The Provincial Government did, indeed, offer to defray Mr Trollope's expenses, but the offer was declined by Mr Trollope."

Prior to Mr Trollope's visit, New Zealand had been the scene of a fierce political controversy. At this time the country was divided into eight Provinces, each of which enjoyed a large measure of self-government, which it wished to retain. There was a growing feeling, however, in the central Government, the New Zealand Parliament, that the best interests of the country would be served by abolition of the Provinces as self-governing units. Mr T. L. Shepherd was a member of the Otago Provincial Council, and also M.P. for Dunstan. As a member of the Council he was expected to oppose the abolition of the Provinces. He had, however, allied himself with the Centralists, was looked upon as a traitor, and incurred the odium of the Otago Provincialists. The Centralists won, and in 1875 the Provinces lost their identity.

A paragraph in the *Otago Witness* of August 17, appears to show that the fire was still smouldering. It provides an interesting example of polite journalistic pleasantries of Victorian days in New Zealand.

"The beauty of the scenery of the Lake district has within the last few days attracted to that region another distinguished

tourist in the person of Mr Anthony Trollope. No doubt Mr
Thomas Luther Shepherd has been cursing his adverse fate
that has led to his being at Wellington, engaged in the arduous
occupation of log-rolling, instead of being at Queenstown to
act the part of showman to Mr Trollope, as he did to Lord
Burghley four years ago. The regret, however, will probably
be all on his side as Mr Trollope will doubtless admit when he
reaches Wellington, and sees the noted legislator. In fact, had
Mr Shepherd been at Queenstown, to force his attentions on
Mr Trollope, the latter gentleman, in his next letter to the
London Daily Telegraph, might have spoken of the Wakatipu
district as Bishop Heber does of Ceylon in his well-known
hymn, 'where every prospect pleases, but only. . . .' "

A quarter of a century after the Trollopes had travelled
through Central Otago in bitter winter weather, and fifteen
years after Anthony had been carried to his grave, a letter
appeared in the *Otago Daily Times* of January 8, 1898, headed
"The Days of Coaching". A correspondent wrote enclosing a
cutting from the *Birmingham Daily Post,* stating that it would
be "interesting to your readers, some of whom may perhaps
remember the incident."

"When Mr Andrew Young, of Wellington, was driving one
of Cobb's coaches somewhere in the wilds of Otago some years
ago, he chanced to drive up against the late Mr Anthony
Trollope, then on his travels. The place where the coach met
Mr Trollope's carriage was in the middle of a narrow cutting
where there was no room to pass. The novelist alighted from
his trap, and with withering scorn addressed the coachman,
ordering him to back his horses to let his own trap pass. 'If you
don't look out of my way in three seconds,' replied Andrew, 'I
will drive my coach and pasengers right over you and your
rattletrap of a one-horse-shay.' 'Sir,' cried the furious novelist,
'do you know who I am?' 'No, I don't; who are you?' said
Andrew. 'My name, sir,' said the great novelist, 'is Anthony
Trollope.' ' Yes, I knew it was some fool or other like that,'
said Andrew. 'Well, Mr Trollope, my name is Andrew Young,
and I give you just one second more, and if you don't start
to back out of this cutting, we'll see your name on a tombstone

as soon as your relatives take the trouble to put it there.' Mr Trollope for once met his match, and without any further attempt at bounce, quietly backed out of the difficulty, and very wisely refrained from recording the incident in his book of travels."

This preposterous story bears its own evidence of absurdity. It implies that Trollope was travelling alone, whereas of course he was accompanied by his wife, and by W. H. Pearson, Commissioner of Crown Lands. Andrew Young may have had such an experience, but certainly not with Anthony Trollope. To crown all, Young was not even in Otago at the time. It is recorded by Lovell-Smith that he left the Province in 1869 to establish a coaching service between Wellington and Wanganui.

There appears to be an element of mystery in the appearance in the *Birmingham Daily Post* of this amusingly fantastic fragment of Trollopiana.

CANTERBURY

FROM OTAGO we went north into the province of Canterbury,—a name which was selected for a then undetermined part of New Zealand. As far as I can ascertain, the Canterbury Association, so called, was first started in 1848, but the idea of such a settlement, to be established in some part of New Zealand, had existed for a considerable time. . . . The settlement was to be made in strict connection with the Church of England, and was to be a model colony. Without a doubt the aspirations which produced first the idea and then the thing were nobly philanthropic. . . . There existed a feeling that something great might be done for a small portion of the British race, by establishing a settlement on an entirely new footing, in which the best of everything English should be retained, English habits of life, English principles, English local government, English freedom, and above all the Church of England.

The scheme had all the merits and all the faults which have attended the fabrication of Utopias, since the benevolence of men has taken the direction. But it has to be acknowledged that they did succeed in creating a prosperous settlement— though the success has not been of the nature which they anticipated. Many of their aspirations have been realised, especially that of so-called responsible local government; but the local government has come, not specially to Canterbury, but to Canterbury as a part of New Zeaand; and not especially to New Zealand, but to New Zealand as one of those thoroughly British dependencies of the mother country which have gradually acquired for themselves the power of parliamentary self-government.

Wakefield and Godley

The two names which are most prominent in the history of the Canterbury settlement are those of John Robert Godley and Edward Gibbon Wakefield. I put that of Godley first, because in truth it was his heart and courage which founded the settlement rather than the head of the man who first formed the plan. Mr Wakefield . . . had been perhaps the author, certainly one of the authors, of the plan by which that colony was originated. His scheme had by no means been fully carried out, and he had conceived great enmity against the officials of the Colonial Office who had not sympathised with his ideas as to the settlement of a colony without any other control from home than that which might be necessary to make it a part of the British empire in reference to foreign affairs.

After reading Mr Wakefield's book and his letters, I cannot think him to have been a good guide for a young colony; but undoubtedly he did hit upon certain truths, the first and chief of which was the inexpediency of bestowing grants of land on colonists, and the wisdom of selling the public lands at a certain fixed price. . . . He was an eager, hard-working, clever man, very energetic in his purpose,—but who, in all his colonising work, seems to have thought more of his own schemes than of the happiness of the colonists whom he proposed to send to their future homes,—and who was quite as anxious to rule his colonists from home by laws made by himself as was ever a Secretary of State in Downing Street.

It was his influence, however, that worked upon Mr Godley,[1] and induced that gentleman to become the real leader of a special band of colonists to New Zealand, Mr Godley, whom I remember as a boy at school thoroughly respected by his

---

1. John Robert Godley (1814-1861). One of the founders of the Canterbury settlement. A fellow-Harrovian with Trollope, who was about a year younger.

school-fellows, seems early in life to have been taught by the Tractarian movement at Oxford that the religion of a community should be the most important consideration. He was a religious man himself, and his friends were men whose thoughts about religion were serious, and whose convictions were sincere. His letters to his friend Mr Adderley[1] have been published,—or at any rate printed and circulated; and no volume of correspondence ever fell into my hands which left upon my mind a higher impression of the purity, piety, philanthropy, truth, and high-minded thoughtfulness of the writer.

Mr Godley had intended to work for the Association at home,—at any rate to remain at that work longer than he did; but in 1849 his health failed him. His chest was weak, his lungs in danger, and his friends recommended that he should leave England for a while. Though the eldest son of a man of property in Ireland, he was himself poor, and therefore some payment for the work of his life was necessary to him. In these circumstances he undertook to proceed to New Zealand as the salaried officer of the Canterbury Association—not as a colonist himself in the usual acceptation of the term, not as one bent on making a new career and a fortune for himself and his children, but as an agent who should busy himself exclusively for the advantage of others. Bearing this in mind he never owned an acre in Canterbury.

Of all the colonists who came with Godley to settle in Christchurch, few probably cared aught about the form of government which might be adopted, caring much, however, caring indeed all in all about the nature of the land on which they were to settle. They would trust to England for freedom with an anxious faith;—but as to the land and the crops which it could bear; as to their future meat and drink and shelter,

---

1. C. B. Adderley (Lord Norton). An under-secretary in the British government.

there were doubt and fear enough, alternate hopes and doubts, —alternate fear and joy. "I am a little puzzled," says Mr Godley, in one of his letters, "as to what ought to be done in political matters. The people are thinking too much just now of getting on their land to care much about attending public demonstrations." No doubt they were. In the meantime Mr Wakefield was earnest at home that the colony should be ruled by Wakefield and not by Earl Grey[1] or any other Secretary of State in Downing Street.

On the 11th April, 1850, the *Lady Nugent,* in which Godley had sailed, came to anchor in Lyttelton Harbour, or Port Cooper, as it was then called. The town of Lyttelton now stands at the head of the harbour named after the nobleman without whose aid the Association could not have made its settlement. The two bold rocks which form the entrance are called Godley Head and Adderley Head. . . . Lyttelton stands down upon a sea inlet, surrounded on every side by mountains, with barely room around it to grow a few potatoes. On the other side of these are the plains which stretch thence to the range which forms the backbone of the Middle Island. These inner hills must have been a sad affliction to the early comers, as their future farms and future city lay beyond them. Mr Godley truly wrote home that the track lay up the side "of what might fairly be called a mountain." I walked it and found it to be a veritable mountain. Now not only has the city of Christchurch been built on the other side, and the farms tilled, and the distant country stocked, but a railway has been made through the mountains from Christchurch to the sea-port, at a cost of £200,000 about a mile and a quarter in

---

1. Sir George Grey, second baronet (1799-1882), grandson of the first Earl Grey. . . . Colonial Secretary in Lord Aberdeen's coalition ministry. Unrelated to Sir George Grey, Governor of **New Zealand.**

length. This tunnel was a gallant undertaking for so young a community.[1]

In his letters Godley says very little about the Church of England characteristic of the settlement. After a while a bishop was found who came out, but did not suit the place, and went back again. After that the present bishop, Dr Harper,[2]—who is now primate of New Zealand,—accepted the see, which he has since administered with success. But there has been no strong Church of England peculiarity about the community. Dr Harper's see, which is, I believe, coterminous with the province of Canterbury, as it was before the Westland goldfields were divided from it, contains a population of 62,158, of which 30,038 are claimed by the Church of England. The proportion is no doubt greater than in the Australian colonies or other parts of New Zealand.

It would have been odd had no results come from the efforts which were made to found a Church of England settlement. But the numbers show the impracticability in these days of dictating to any community the religious convictions by which it shall be guided. In a few years the very idea of Canterbury being specially the province of one denomination will be lost to the memory of the colonists themselves,—unless indeed it be perpetuated by the huge record of their failure which the town of Christchurch contains. In the centre of it there is a large waste space in which £7,000 have been buried in laying the foundations of a cathedral;—but there is not a single stone or a single brick above the level of the ground. The idea of building the cathedral is now abandoned.

---

1. The Port Hills have recently been pierced by a second tunnel for road transport.
2. Bishop H. J. C. Harper (1804-1893). His see at first included Otago as well, until Bishop Nevill's arrival at Dunedin in 1871.

It was a sad sight to me to look down upon the vain foundations.[1]

Opposite the spot where the door would have been, stands a statue, by Woolner, of my old schoolfellow,—the great ornament of the city of Christchurch. Judging from portraits of the man, the likeness is excellent, though the artist never saw his subject. The statue itself which was known to many Englishmen before it came out to New Zealand, is very noble. Among modern statues, I know no head that stands better on its shoulders.

Godley came home to England, held high office for some years in the Civil Service, and died on November 17, 1861, of the disease which had made his journey to New Zealand a necessity. Of a better or more earnest man I do not remember to have read the record.

I cannot finish this short notice of one of those men, who with true energy and in a real spirit of philanthropy instituted the colony of Canterbury, without making some reference to another of the body, without whom Canterbury must have been a failure. This I may perhaps best do by quoting a passage from a speech made at Christchurch, on February 6, 1858, at a breakfast given to Lord Lyttelton[2] and Mr Selfe[3], who were then visiting the colony with which their names are so intimately associated. Mr T. [J.] E. Fitzgerald[4], than whom no New Zealand colonist is better known, in proposing the

---

1. By the following year the "Pilgrims" had begun to climb out of the Slough of Despond. In 1873 the building was begun, and completed in 1881 at a cost of £50,000. In later years it was added to, and is the dominant feature of the "Cathedral City."

2. A founder and benefactor of Canterbury.

3. H. S. Selfe. Provincial agent in London for Canterbury. One of the founders who assisted the settlement financially.

4. James Edward Fitzgerald (1818-1896). Pioneer of Canterbury, and Provincial Superintendent 1853-1857.

Buckingham 8 Augst 72

Waltham House,
Waltham Cross.

My dear Mr Fitzgerald

Thanks for the sheets.
I have already cut out a
portion of the for publication,
— which I hope is not
in opposition to your wishes.
Personally I do not
like Lord Lytton; but
I think him a good man,
and I am anxious
to but on record my
opinion of his loan to
the

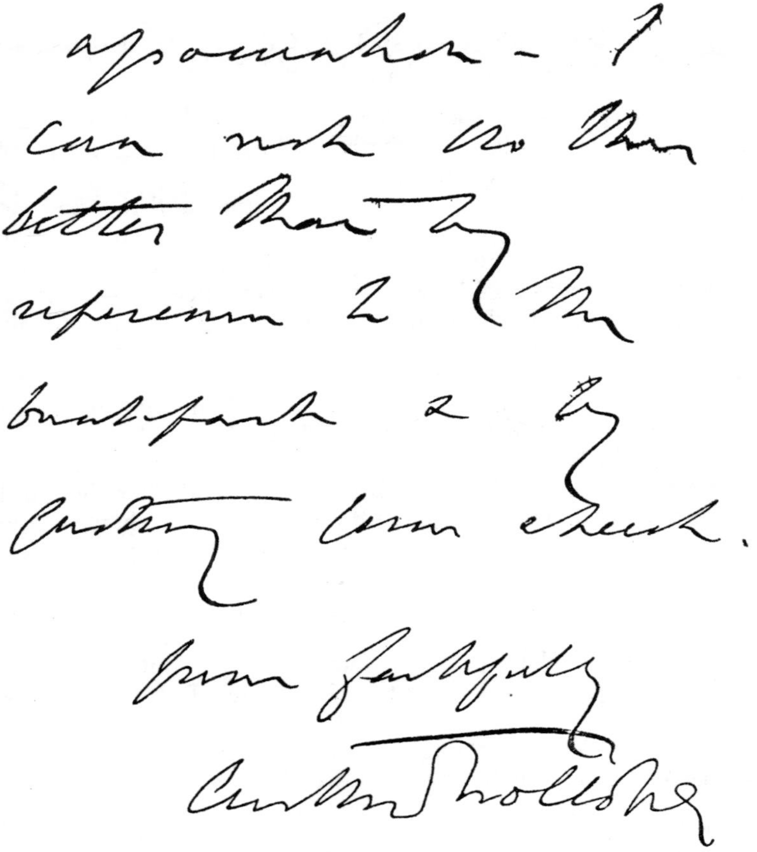
appreciation – I
can wish no other
better than my
experience of the
breakfast & my
Christmas [illegible] [illegible].
Yours faithfully
Anthony Trollope

Trollope's letter to J. E. FitzGerald, Christchurch, concerning FitzGerald's eulogy of Lord Lyttelton. (Original in Alexander Turnbull Library, Wellington.)

health of their English guests, spoke as follows of Lord Lyttelton;
—and spoke with accurate truth.

" I well remember, soon after I first joined the Canterbury
Association, and when we were falling into all kinds of
difficulties when we had no money to pay our agent's expenses
in the colony, when bills were coming due and we had no
funds to meet them, and when in fact there began to have
every appearance of an awful failure—I well remember, after
a long conversation with Mr Gibbon Wakefield, going down
to consult Lord Lyttelton, and appearing before him suddenly
at eleven o'clock at night at Brighton. The result was that his
Lordship came up at once to London and took charge of the
affairs of the Canterbury Association; and from that time, and
for a long time afterwards laboured in those affairs as few
men ever did labour in any public office. Without the smallest
prospect of remuneration, he advanced thousand after thousand
of pounds to keep the settlement going till the time should come
when its own funds would be available. The very roads on
which some of you may have worked were made out of funds
supplied out of the pockets of two or three members of the
Canterbury Association, of whom Lord Lyttelton was the
foremost. [Loud cheers]. It is a fact of which Canterbury may
be justly proud—nay, without which none of us could dare
to show our faces here today—that the debt thus incurred
has been repaid; but though the money has been repaid we
can never forget the feeling with which it was advanced, nor
cease to remember how much we owe to the generous self-
sacrificing spirit which carried the colony in safety through the
difficulties that beset the first year of its existence."

On crossing the Waitaki River in the manner I have
described . . . we found ourselves in the province of Canterbury,
and among the people,—very few and far between for the
first few miles of our journey,—who are still called the
Canterbury Pilgrims. The precise spirit of the name will be
easily understood. The founders of the colony,—for it was in
truth a separate colony created with a distinct settlement of
its own,—came out with the express idea of forming a religious
community, and were thus entitled to be called pilgrims. The

name of the chosen locality was assumed as having a special
Church of England savour, and thus a happy old combination
was revived, which from different causes sounded pleasantly
in the ears of the educated men and women who had determined
to make this part of New Zealand their future home.

From the Waitaki to Christchurch, the capital of Canterbury,
was a journey of two days, through the towns of Waimoti
[Waimate] and Timaru. The rivers here form the chief
peculiarity of the country, which when flooded by rains or by
melting snow form one broad and rapid course. They are for
the most part unbridged, and therefore at certain times
impassable[1]. Over one river with apparently endless different
courses, called the Rangitata, we were preceded by a horseman
who for his services charged us 2s apiece. Over another, the
Rakaia, the first elements of a railway bridge had been constructed, and we were taken over by a truck dragged by a
horse who kept the bed of the river where it was dry or the
water shallow, and ascended to the level of the frail-looking
bridge where the stream was deep. The whole thing looked
like sudden death[2]—but we reached the other side of the Rakaia
in safety, and were only charged 2s a head for all that was
done for us. It may be taken as a rule that rivers in Canterbury
cost so much and no more.

During our whole journey from the Waitaki to Christchurch,
we were crossing the Canterbury Plains,—of the fertility of
which so much has been heard in England. It is an uninteresting
journey as far as scenery is concerned. To the left the great
range of mountains which runs throughout the island was
always in sight with its snow-capped peaks,—somewhat relieving
the dullness of the plain,—but they are not sufficiently near to

---

1. All these rivers were bridged a few years later.
2. One of the most dangerous rivers before it was bridged.
   Travellers had sometimes to wait days before crossing was
   possible.

create landscape beauty. To the right was the sea, often close
at hand during the first day, but seldom visible. We passed
on from one squatter's home to another, through vast paddocks
containing perhaps 20,000 acres each, without a tree[1]. The
grass consisted of long coarse tussocks—brown in colour,—with
nothing of green prettiness to relieve the monotony. To the
eye it certainly was not charming, but I had already learned
enough of sheep[2] to know that as a pastoral country it was
good. I was told that it would carry two sheep to three acres.
Any pastures that will do that on aboriginal grasses must be
very good. I had thought that we should pass through more
cultivated ground than I saw on the road. Indeed I had
expected to find the Canterbury plains one vast expanse of
corn-bearing land. This is by no means the case. Owing to
the course which the road takes the traveller sees little of
agriculture, except in the neighbourhood of Timaru, till he
reaches Selwyn, within a few miles of Christchurch. For this
there are two apparent reasons. The land which has been
purchased for tillage at a distance from Christchurch, lies
chiefly on the river beds, and has been taken up with reference
to water frontages. It runs, therefore, in strips down from the
mountains to the sea, and does not meet the traveller's eyes.
And then the squatters have found it worth their while to buy
large tracts of land for pastoral purpose,—so as to keep free
selectors and farmers at a distance.

The price of land under the Canterbury Association was at
first £3 an acre,—and at this rate the land round Christchurch
was sold to the first settlers, by those who bought it from the
New Zealand Land Company on behalf of the Association.
The price was then reduced to 10s an acre, at which rate
much of what was then considered the distant districts of

---

1. No longer a treeless plain, the landscape has been transformed,
   and the large runs subdivided into smaller allotments.
2. In Australia Trollope had visited his son, a sheep farmer.

the province was alienated to a few happy capitalists. But for some years past the price for all land in the province has been £2 an acre. For £2 an acre any man who can pay the money down may purchase as many sections as he desires containing twenty acres each,—and he may pick the sections as he pleases, buying a bit here and a bit there,—a practice which in Australia they call picking the eyes out of "the country,"—and one which the framers of the land laws in the different Australian colonies have done their best to prevent. In Canterbury it is urged that at the higher price thus exacted for land,—40s an acre in lieu of 20s or less, with ready money in lieu of deferred payments,—the colony can afford to welcome any purchasers picking out the best land, and that purchasers picking out the best land, and thus opening up the country, will soon be followed by others who will content themselves with the second-best,—and so on. I have heard many lengthened arguments on both sides of the question,—with which I will not trouble my readers. Each colony may perhaps be fairly presumed to know what mode of sale will suit its own circumstances. In the excellence of its land Canterbury has been very happy, and as a consequence of that excellence, it is second in achieved success to no colony sent out from Great Britain.

The majority of the land bought of late has been purchased by squatters, and not by farmers or free selectors. In the year ended the 30th June, 1872, run-holders—or squatters,—bought 23,184 acres in the province, and other persons, who no doubt all purchased as farmers, bought 17,807 acres. The figures are interesting as showing the progressive nature of pastoral pursuits in New Zealand. No squatter in New South Wales or Queensland can afford to pay 40s an acre on which to run sheep,— nor even 20s. . . . But in New Zealand the purchaser lays down artificial grasses, and in a few years is able to carry five, six or seven sheep, instead of perhaps half a sheep to an acre. In every province of New Zealand which I visited,—and I visited them all except Hawke Bay [Hawkes Bay],—I saw English grasses in profusion, and English-looking fields. In Australia English grasses have no doubt been introduced, but I have never seen the side of a mountain covered with them, as I have in New Zealand. The cause of this is to be found in the climate. In New Zealand it seems that everything thrives which ever throve in England. The Southern,—or Middle,—Island, is a second England, only with higher mountains, bigger lakes, and rougher shores. She has indeed gold instead of iron and coal[1], and is in that respect much the poorer country of the two.

The province of Canterbury already supports large quantities of grain, assisting to feed all the other provinces of New Zealand, and occasionally exporting wheat to Victoria and England. The ports from which it is sent are Lyttelton and Timaru. The first object of a colony should be to grow enough wheat for itself,—if it be placed in a country capable of growing wheat. New Zealand in the year 1871 exported wheat and flour to the value of £75,156,—but imported to the value of £127,040,—showing a deficiency of £51,164. But the province of Canterbury, in regard to the production of wheat, holds her head high. Not only does she supply the greater portion of the breadstuffs exported from New Zealand to other countries, but largely helps to supply her weaker sister provinces. In 1870 she supplied the other provinces with corn and flour to the value of £137,000, and in the first six months of 1871 to the value of £50,800.

---

1. "There is coal in the Middle Island. In Otago they burn a kind of coal by no means of a pleasant nature, which they call lignite. Coal has been found also at Nelson, but has not hitherto been profitably worked." (A. T's. Note).

There is good coal at Kaitangata, Otago. Westport coal won fame for New Zealand in 1889. At Apia, on March 15, a furious hurricane drove a number of ships ashore. H.M.S. *Calliope* alone escaped destruction when her commander took her out to sea in the teeth of the storm, aided by Westport coal with which her bunkers were loaded.

Beginnings of railways, with railway rumours, railway prophecies, and railway fears, met us everywhere on our passage up the islands. It must always be remembered that these colonial railways are not private speculations as they are with us, but are constructed,—or to be constructed,—with money borrowed by the colony for the purpose. If it be calculated that the money can be borrowed at 5 percent, and that the expected traffic will pay for the working of the railway,—two positions for which the advocates of the New Zealand railway system take for granted,—then the question is this: Will the value of railway communication to the colony be worth the interest which the colony must pay for the money borrowed? Any partisan could talk by the hour,—if given to talking, or write by the chapter,—if given to writing, either on one side or the other; or first on one side and then on the other. Facts can prove nothing in the matter, and speculation must carry the day either on that side or on this. That a national debt is a grievous burden to a young country is of course not to be denied. That railways running through a country, at present deficient in roads, will increase trade and add greatly to the value of the land and to the value of the produce of the land, is equally manifest. Such a question in a community governed by free institutions, representative parliaments, and responsible ministers, at last becomes one of partisan politics.

There will be the borrowing and spending side of the House, the members of which will be great in their oratory on behalf of progress,—and there will be the cautious side of the House, which would fain be just before it is generous, whose oratory will be equally great in denouncing the reckless audacity of the spendthrifts. The borrowing and spending side will generally have some great prophet of its own who can look far into the future, who can see ample returns to the community for any amount of expenditure, who is himself fond of political power, and who can see at any rate this,—that the great body of voters in the country, on whom he must depend for his power, are for the most part indifferent to future circumstances, so long as money at the moment be spent in profusion. When I reached New Zealand Mr Vogel was the great prophet of the hour,—and under his auspices money had been largely borrowed, and great contracts has been given for railways which are ultimately to run through the two islands from The Bluff [Bluff] up to Auckland and north of Auckland. Of Mr Vogel and his fate[1], while I was in the colony, I shall have to say a few words when speaking of the parliament at Wellington; but I have found it impossible to touch the subject of railways in New Zealand without mentioning the name of a man who I was assured by one party will hereafter be regarded as the great promoter of the success of his adopted country,—or, as I was assured, by another party, be denounced as her ruin.

At Selwyn we got upon one of these beginnings of railways, which took us into Christchurch, a distance of twenty-three miles, through one of the richest districts of the settlement. Christchurch as a town is certainly not magnificent, but it is comfortable and thoroughly English. The houses are chiefly of wood,—as are also the greater number of the churches. The banks here, as elsewhere, luxuriate in stone. Throughout all these colonies I have grudged the grandeur of the banks, being reminded by every fine facade of percentages, commission, and charges for exchange. I believe that in Australia and New Zealand a man might melt his money down to nothing quicker

---

1. Sir Julius Vogel (1835-1899). In 1873 he became Prime Minister, and was knighted in 1876. To him New Zealand owes the Government Life Insurance Department, the Public Trust Office, the Land Transfer Title. He arrived in New Zealand in 1861, and was a founder of the *Otago Daily Times,* New Zealand's first daily newspaper. He lost favour in Otago by advocating the abolition of the provinces.

than anywhere else simply by transferring it from one place to another. I feel myself to be ill-natured in saying this, as personally I received great courtesy from the bankers;—but not the less did I find the melting process was the practice.

Christchurch as a city is certainly much less imposing than Dunedin. The population of the city is about 8,000[1],—that of the electoral districts of Christchurch, is something over 12,000. The special religious tenets of the founders of the colony may be gathered perhaps more clearly from the names of the streets than from any other characteristic which a stranger will observe. They are all named after some Church of England bishopric; —and in the choosing of the special dioceses which were to be so honoured, there has certainly been no mean time-serving, no special worship of the great ones of the Church. The Irish Church has been specially honoured, for there are Armagh Street, Tuam Street and Cashel Street. There are also Gloucester Street, Lichfield Street, and Hereford Street, and St. Asaph Street. But there is no York Street, or London Street, or Winchester Street. There is, however, an Antigua Street, a Barbadoes Street, and a Montreal Street; and the chief street of all is Colombo Street.[2]

I have already spoken of the failure of the Canterbury pilgrims in reference to the building of a cathedral. . . . I could not but be melancholy as I learned that the honest high-toned idea of the honest high-toned founders of the colony would

---

1. The population of Christchurch is now (1969) over a quarter of a million. . . . It overtook Dunedin, and is the second largest city in New Zealand.

2. The Christchurch streets were named by the pioneer surveyors, Captain Joseph Thomas and Edward Jollie. The streets of Lyttelton were first named, followed by Sumner. "The result," wrote Jollie, "was that these two towns had used up most of the tip-top titles, and for Christchurch, which came last, there was scarcely anything left but Ireland and the colonies."

probably not be carried out; but perhaps on that spot in the middle of the city a set of public offices will be better than a cathedral. Public offices all the community will use. A cathedral will satisfy something less than one half of it;—and will greatly dissatisfy the other half. Such a church, by its site, by its magnificence, by the very zeal of those who are hot in its erection, proclaims ascendency;—and if there be one feeling more repugnant than any other to the genuine British colonist, it is that of Church ascendency. Many of the settlers have come away from their old homes in order that they may be rid of it. It savours to them of tyranny and priest-rule. They do not dislike the worship of the Church of England,—perhaps they prefer it on the whole to any other. Statistics show that it is still more popular than any other one form of worship in the colonies. But colonists as a body are averse to any assertion that one Church is by its own merits deserving of higher outward honour than another. The name of a cathedral may be innocent enough,—but the builders of them in the colonies should, I think, for the present make them large only in accordance with the wants of their flocks. In Christchurch there is no doubt a disappointed feeling of ungratified ascendency.

Canterbury has a Parliament of its own, as has Otago,— and in Christchurch there still exists a hope, as there does also in Dunedin, that a good time is coming in which the General Assembly may be moved south from favoured Wellington to its own halls,—if only for a time[1]. . . . The hall in which the Provincial Council of Canterbury sits is spacious and very handsome, and I was told that it was built with a view to accommodate the Colonial House of Representatives. I was assured afterwards at Wellington, that the question of such a journey southwards was still considered to be open. The hall

---

1. There has never since been any serious suggestion of removing the seat of Government from Wellington.

in question is perhaps a little too highly coloured, but is certainly very fine. I was accompanied by a member of the Provincial Council, who admitted that it had one slight drawback. Those who spoke in it could not make themselves heard. I myself had no opportunity of testing it, as the General Assembly was sitting at Wellington while I was in the colony, and the General Assembly and the Provincial Councils never sit together. This hall forms part of a set of buildings erected for the management of the affairs of the province, which as a whole pleased me very much. It is partly of stone and partly of wood, but is Gothic throughout, the woodwork being as graceful and as true to the design of the whole as the stone. It stands on the banks of the little river Avon, which meanders through the town, having a few willows on the bank, with a wooden footbridge[1]. The buildings form a quadrangle, and look as though one of the smaller and prettier colleges had been transplanted thither from the banks of the Cam. As I stood and looked at it I could not but think that some exiled member of the university may some day have consoled himself with the same feeling.

I found that allotments of land for building purposes within a mile or two of the town were worth from £50 to £150 an acre. In all these towns the great proportion of comfortable villa residences to poor and squalid cottages is very striking. Indeed there are no poor or squalid cottages. All round Christchurch there are houses which in the neighbourhood of an English country town would devote an expenditure of £500 or £600 a year, and which here certainly cannot be maintained at a lesser rate. The one great complaint made by the ladies who occupy these houses,—the one sorrow indeed of the

---

1. The banks on either side of the Avon, planted with a variety of trees, flower beds and lawns, now form one of the most picturesque of the amenities of Christchurch.

matrons of New Zealand,—arises from the dearth of maid-servants. Sometimes no domestic servant can be had at all, for love or money, and the matron of the house with her daughters, if she have any, are constrained to cook the dinner and make the beds. Sometimes a lass who knows nothing will consent to come into a house and be taught how to do house-work at the rate of £40 per annum, with a special proviso that she is to be allowed to go out two evenings a week to learn choral singing in the music-hall. By more than two or three ladies my sympathy was demanded on account of these sufferings, and I was asked whether a country must not be in a bad way in which the ordinary comfort of female attendance could not be had when it was wanted. Of course I sympathised. It is hard upon a pretty young mother with three or four children that she should be left to do everything for herself. But I could not help suggesting that the young woman's view of the case was quite as important as the matron's, and that if it was a bad place for those who wanted to hire maid-servants, it must be a very good place for the girls who wanted to be hired. The maid-servant's side of the question is quite as important as the mistress's. The truth is, that in such a town as Christchurch, a girl of twenty or twenty-three can earn from £40 to £60 a year and a comfortable home, with no oppressively hard work; and if she be well-conducted and of decent appearance she is sure to get a husband who can keep a house over her head. For such persons New Zealand is paradise. It is not only that they get so many more of the good things of the world than would ever come in their way in England, but that they stand relatively in so much higher a position in reference to the world around them. The very tone in which a maid-servant speaks to you in New Zealand, her quiet little joke, her familiar smile, her easy manner, tell you at once that the badge of servitude is not heavy on her. She takes your wages, and makes your bed, and hands your plate,

—but she does not consider herself to be of an order of beings different from your order. Many who have been accustomed to be served all their life may not like this. If so they had better not live in New Zealand. But if we look at the matter from the maid-servant's side, we cannot fail to find that there is much comfort in it.

I would advise no young lady to go out to any colony either to get a husband, or to be a governess, or to win her bread after any so-called lady-like fashion. She may suffer much before she can succeed, or may probably fail altogether. But any well-behaved young woman who now earns £16 as a housemaid in England would find in New Zealand a much happier home.

I must say a word about the museum at Christchurch, though museums are things of which I am very ignorant. I was taken to the museum by the curator, Dr Haast[1], to see the skeletons of curious moas, in the arrangement and reconstruction of which he is a great authority. There is a little world there of moas and kiwis, and a collection of large stones which the moas have swallowed, as other birds pick up gravel to assist digestion, and of eggs which the kiwis have laid almost as big as themselves. Next to the Maoris, who are not as yet quite extinct[2], the moas, which are, must be regarded as the most remarkable productions of New Zealand. They fed upon grass, with stones an inch in diameter to assist their digestion. They were twelve feet high, and seem at one time to have had the islands almost to themselves. In the museum are various clusters of their broken bones,—of bones which have been found broken; and from these fractures Dr Haast draws the conclusion that there were, before the Maoris, a race of moa-

1. Later Sir Julius von Haast (1822-1887). Explorer and scientist. Founder of the Christchurch Museum.
2. The Maori population is increasing at a higher rate than that of European stock.

hunters, who regaled themselves with the marrow which was thus obtained. I do not express doubt of the correctness of his view. I never do doubt the facts which science proclaims to me. But I found men in New Zealand who would not believe in the moa-hunters. In the museum there is a portrait of Gibbon Wakefield and his dogs, portions of which are said to have been painted by Landseer. The statue of Godley is at a little distance outside,—and is as much superior to the picture as the character and attributes of the man sculptured were greater than those of him who was painted[1].

The appearance of the country around Christchurch is especially English. The land is divided into small English-looking fields, with English grasses, and English hedges. In regard to the hedges, it may be well to remark that the gorse, which has been brought over from England and acclimatised, has taken so kindly to its new home that it bids fair to become a monstrous pest. It spreads itself wide over the land and lanes, and unless periodically clipped claims the soil as its own. But each periodical clipping, with rural labour at 6s a day is a serious addition to the expense of farming.

Lyttelton is the port by which Christchurch imports and exports what it buys and what it produces; and between

---

1. Of Edward Gibbon Wakefield (1796-1862) the *Dictionary of National Biography* had this to say: "The importance of Wakefield's achievements in colonial matters can hardly be over-estimated. The tangible fruits of his labours are the least part of their result, for all subsequent colonial development has followed the direction of his thought. He brought to the subject for the first time the mind of a philosopher and statesman equally fitted for framing a comprehensive theory and for directing its working in practical detail. The great flaw in his character was lack of scruple in selecting the means for attaining his ends. This imperfection of character brought about serious disaster in his private affairs, and in his public life it prevented even his most devoted supporters from giving him their implicit confidence."

Christchurch and Port Lyttelton there is a mountain so steep as almost to defy traffic. When the first Canterbury pilgrims landed at Port Lyttelton their courage for new adventure must almost have passed away from them, when they perceived that the settlers in the plain beyond the mountains would be divided by such a barrier from the sea. A road has indeed been made over the barrier, not so steep but what a horse may travel it, and round from the harbour there is a tedious navigation by the channel of the Heathcote River nearly up to Christchurch. But neither of these modes of transit suffices to put a town into comfortable communication with the sea. Consequently the Canterbury folk determined to make a railway, and in doing so have carried a tunnel through the mountain, a distance of a mile and three-quarters, at an expense amounting to £200,000. It was a great enterprise for so small a community, and was absolutely essential to the well-being of Christchurch as a town. There can be no doubt, however, that the tunnel has doubled the value of the land lying immediately on the inland side of the hills. Port Lyttelton itself is a very picturesque place, hemmed in on every side by hills, at the head of a narrow land-locked bay, with the mountains of Banks's[1] Peninsula standing over it.

I must say a word of the county of Westland before I have done with Canterbury,—of Westland and its capital, Hokitika[2], which till 1868 were comprised within the province of Canterbury. Hokitika is a thriving gold-town, on the western coast, and is the centre of various gold-fields. When gold "broke out," as the phrase goes, on the western side of the Middle Island, and when the rush to Hokitika, together with the export of gold from Hokitika, became a great matter, the pastoral and agricultural province of Canterbury, not caring to maintain

---

1. Now known as Banks Peninsula.
2. Hokitika has since been far outstripped by Greymouth, the chief town of Westland today.

an alliance with interests so different from those to which it was accustomed, severed itself from the gold-fields[1]. Then the name of Westland was assumed, and Westland became, not exactly a province, but a county independent of any other province, with municipal institutions of its own. Time did not admit of my crossing the island from Canterbury, to the west coast, so that I saw nothing of the glories of Hokitika,—to my infinite regret. For though the district is famous for its gold, it is, if possible, more famous for its scenery. It lies under Mount Cook, the monarch of New Zealand mountains, less, but only less in altitude than its brother monarch in Europe. I had heard much of the beauty of the road across the island, much of the scenery around Mount Cook and its glaciers, and I had determined to visit them. But Australia and New Zealand together cover a wide space,—and I was obliged to give up the west coast of the Middle Island. Of course to my dying day the conviction will haunt me that when in New Zealand I did not see the one thing best worth seeing in the colony[2].

---

1. Separation from Canterbury was mainly due to agitation on the part of Westlanders, who became dissatisfied with their attachment to Canterbury, and desired a greater measure of independence.

2. Trollope evidently had in mind the Fox and Franz Josef glaciers. The Fox Glacier was named for Sir William Fox. The Franz Josef was named by its discoverer, von Haast, in honour of the then Emperor of Austria. This glacier descends through the bush to within a few hundred feet of sea level. The Fox-Franz Josef area is one of the highlights of the highway which now crosses the Southern Alps at Arthur's Pass in the north and Haast Pass in the south, connecting Westland both with Canterbury and Otago.

What did Canterbury Think of Anthony Trollope?

SILENCE OF THE PRESS

Rather strangely, the Trollopes appear to have arrived at Christchurch, spent about a week, and departed with scarcely a nod of recognition from the press. On Friday, August 16, it was reported in *The Press* that Trollope had sent a telegram to a friend (whose identity was not mentioned), stating that he was leaving Dunedin that day for Christchurch. The three days' coach journey would have brought him to Christchurch on the Sunday, and the next reference to him occurs a week later, when it was reported that he had left Lyttelton by the *Alhambra* for Wellington.

Of his week in Canterbury, Trollope mentions but one resident whom he personally met, though there are passing references to Bishop Harper, J. E. FitzGerald and H. S. Selfe. He tells us that Dr (later Sir Julius von) Haast conducted him through the Museum.

Marlborough and Nelson

ROM PORT LYTTELTON we went by steamer to Wellington, the political capital of the colony, which is situated at the southern extremity of the Northern Island; but as we touched at Picton, in the province of Marlborough, and at Nelson, in the province of that name, on our journey from Wellington northwards to Auckland, and as those two provinces are in the Middle Island, it may be well that I should take them first. I am entitled to say but little about them, as I did in fact but just touch them. . . .

The journey from Wellington to Nelson, through Cook's [Cook] Strait, which divides the two islands, is very picturesque, especially if the steamer take Picton in its course. The headlands and broken bays, with the rough steep mountains coming sheer down into the blue waters, the closeness of the land, and the narrowness of the passages, all tend to create a mysterious charm, which he who gazes at them finds himself unable to analyse. He feels tempted to land at every gully which runs up among the mountains and to investigate the strange wild world which must be beyond them. He knows, in truth, that there is nothing there,—that one brown hill would lead only to another, that there is no life among the hills, and that the very spots on which his eyes rest, really contain whatever there may be of loveliness in the place. But though he knows this as fact, his imagination will not allow him to trust his knowledge. There is always present to him a vague longing to investigate the mysteries of the valleys, and to penetrate into the bosoms of the distant hills. The sweetest charms of landscape are as those of life;—they consist of the anticipations of something beyond

which never can be reached. I never felt this more strongly
than when I was passing from one land-locked channel to
another along the coast of Cook's Strait.

Marlborough

We left Wellington during the night and at six in the morning
we were entering Tory Channel on the opposite island, so called
from the name of the vessel in which Wakefield's first party of
emigrants arrived. From thence we passed into Queen
Charlotte's Sound[1] at the top of which is the little town of
Picton, which till lately was the capital of the province of
Marlborough. I believe it still considers itself to be so[2], but the
Provincial Council,—the presence of which I presume to be
the truest mark of a New Zealand capital,—has been removed
to the other town which the province possesses, called Blenheim.
Neither of these places has as yet a population of 1,000
inhabitants, but the whole province, by the census of 1871,
possessed no more than 5,235 souls, and yet in 1860, when
the number was very much less, the people of the district found
it essential to their well-being to separate themselves from the
province of Nelson. The land in those parts, they said, was
sold by the Nelson Council or the Nelson Executive, and the
money forthcoming from the land was spent in Nelson, instead
of being used to open up the country which produced it. As
to the expedience or inexpedience of the change, I have no
opinion,—but it strikes an Englishman as strange that a scattered
community of a few thousand persons spread among the
mountains should require a separate government for themselves,
—with a separate parliament, and all the attendant expenses.
I could not, however, but remember how I had been myself

1. Queen Charlotte Sound. Named by Captain Cook in January
   1770.
2. The early controversy over the site of the capital has long been
   happily forgotten. Blenheim has by far the larger population.

convinced of the necessity of separating the Riverina from New South Wales, for the very reasons which caused the separation of Marlborough from Nelson, and I was disposed to think that the people of Marlborough may have been right. . . . Marlborough carried its point,—and Picton became a capital, among New Zealand capitals, till further jealousy removed its honours to Blenheim. Small as Marlborough is in numbers, there is a smaller province, that of Taranaki, of which I shall speak by-and-by.

At Picton I found the son of an English friend, who himself had been among the earliest of the New Zealand settlers, superintending the erection of a railway from thence to Blenheim,—a railway with about 700 people at each end of it, and which may perhaps benefit in some remote way an entire population of 2,000 or 3,000! The financial ministers of New Zealand have certainly been very brave. Navvies, I found, had been brought out from England under contracts to work for a certain time at certain rates; but, of course, these contracts were ignored by the men when they found, or thought that they had found, that they could do better for themselves by ignoring them. It is absolutely useless for any employer of labour to take labour out to the colonies for his own use, paying the expense of the transit. Unwilling services are of all services the dearest, and such services if they be kept at all are sure to be unwilling.

Picton itself is a pretty, straggling, picturesque little town, lying as do all these New Zealand ports, pressed in between the mountains and the sea. It is a strangely isolated place, with no road anywhere but to its rival Blenheim. Once a week from Wellington, and once from Neson, a steamer touches there, and thus it holds its communication with the world. How it lives I could not find out. The staple of the province is wool, and it owns ever 600,000 sheep,—about as many as all Western Australia possesses,—but Nelson is not the port at

which the wool is shipped. That goes down to another bay, near
to Blenheim. It is hard to discover how such towns do live, as
700 persons can hardly make their bread by trading on each
otner; and as they import their clothes, their brandy, their
tobacco, and, I am sorry so say their wheat also, they must
produce something wherewith to purchase these good things.
Whilst navvies are earning 6s or 7s a day by making a railway,
I can understand that trade should go on. The wages of the
men fall into the little town like manna from heaven. But such
a fall of manna as that is apt to come to a speedy end. As far
as outward appearances go, Picton seemed to be doing very
well. There were good shops and tidy houses, and pretty gardens,
and a general look of sleepy, well-fed prosperity. In all these
places the people are well fed and well clothed, whatever may
be the sources from whence the food and raiment come. I may
say also that Picton enjoys a beautiful climate, produces all
English fruits in rich abundance, is surrounded by fields
deliciously green, and has for an immediate background some
of the finest scenery in New Zealand. . . .

Nelson

From Picton we came back through Queen Charlotte's Sound,
up Admiralty Bay, which is another of the wonderful land-
locked harbours with which the coast is indented, and through
the French Pass[1], as it is called, on to Nelson. Admiralty Bay
is not in fact an indentation of the land, but is formed by
D'Urville's [D'urville] Island, and the French Pass is a very
narrow channel,—made doubly interesting by a fatal rock in
the very centre of it,—between the island and the main land.
It is all very well now for steamers with charts and coal and

---

1. Dumont D'Urville was the first to venture through this narrow
   pass, in 1827, in his corvette *Astrolabe*.

all nautical appliances, but one is lost in wonder at the audacity of the men when one thinks of the work which such sailors as Tasman and Cook were called on to perform.

Nelson is a settlement which has attracted much more attention at home than has been paid to Picton. Few parts of New Zealand, indeed, were oftener made the subject of conversation in England some years back than the settlement of Nelson. It has a bishop[1], too, of its own,—a sturdy clergyman of the right sort for such a position, who looks as though he had been created to manage the clergy of a colonial diocese,—a man who can put the collar on his own horse, or ride fifty miles at a stretch, or hold his own in any conflict either by word or hand. A colonial bishop should be hale, vigorous, young, and good-humoured, ready to preach, to laugh, or to knock a fellow down at any moment. But when I say this I do not forget thee, thou best of all bishops that now in these latter days wearest an apron, though thou too art colonial and hast held thy charge till years are creeping on thee, so that thou canst now hardly knock down any man except by argument. Old schoolfellow, how pleasant thou wert to me when thou spokest of former things,—and how urgent for good, how strong in faith, how pugnacious, and yet how gentle! After I know not how many years of rough and battling life in a rough and battling colony thou wert still the English gentleman fresh from his college. Did it every occur to thee how great to me was the relish of thy decorous pleasantries? . . .

Nelson was first settled by the New Zealand Land Company in 1841. . . . The air was pleasant, the scene was beautiful

---

1. Edmund Hobhouse (1817-1904). Consecrated 1858. He visited every corner of his wide bishopric on horseback or on foot—a man after Trollope's own heart. The description appears to fit Hobhouse, but when the novelist visited New Zealand he had been succeeded by Bishop Suter, then only about forty. Hobhouse had retired and returned to England. Is Trollope's later reference related to that period?

around them, the harbour though difficult of entrance was secure, and though there was snow on the mountains close around them, there were sweet flowers on the plain, and good herbage. When subsequently, in 1843, a report was made to the government by the land commissioner who had been appointed to enquire for how much land the New Zealand Land Company had really given value to the natives, it was decided that at Nelson 151,000 acres had been fairly purchased, —and on that amount of territory, which would have been amply sufficient for their purpose had there been no beautiful but barren mountains, the settlers made themselves a home, and established Nelson, by no means the least important of the New Zealand provinces. . . . The town contains 6,000 people, and the province something over 22,000. I was told that the land was good, but light and worn out from continual cropping, that nearly all the land in the province available for agriculture was sold; that farming or at any rate growing wheat, did not pay, unless a man could get his work done by the inmates of his own family; and that there was but slight material prosperity in the place. One or two men might be making fortunes,—but for the rest Nelson was a slow spot. There was no money there and no enterprise. They did not even grow wheat enough for themselves, though they professed to be an agricultural community. There was certainly a sleepiness about the place when regarded from commercial eyes.

But though sleepy, it appeared to be happy. I was there about the beginning of September,—a winter month[1],—and nothing could be sweeter or more pleasant than the air. The summer heats are not great, and all English fruits, and grass, and shrubs grow at Nelson with more than English profusion. Every house was neat and pretty. The site is, I think, as lovely

---

1. In September winter is giving way to spring. Nelson and Blenheim vie with each other for the greatest number of hours of sunshine per year in New Zealand.

as that of any town I ever saw. Merely to breathe there, and to dream, and to look around was a delight. Nobody seemed to be either rich or poor,—to be either great or humble. They have their own Parliament House, and their own parliament, and manage themselves after a sleepy, fat and plentiful rather than prosperous fashion, which is not without its advantages in the world. The children are generally well-taught,—and certainly should be so, as there is nothing to pay for education. Every householder pays £1 per annum towards the school, and for every child between five and fifteen the parents pay 5s a year, whether the child be at school or not. The payments are made as a matter of course, and the children are educated.

I was very much in love with Nelson during the few hours that I passed there; but it is not the place to which I would send a young man to make a fortune.

Trollope and the Nelson Press

There appears to be no press record of the brief visit of Mr and Mrs Trollope to Nelson, though on Wednesday, August 28, the *Nelson Examiner* announced that "Mr and Mrs Anthony Trollope, who were passengers by the Alhambra, will, during their stay in Wellington, be the guests of His Excellency the Governor", and on Saturday, September 14, the people of Nelson were informed that, at Auckland, "Mr Anthony Trollope is the guest of Dr Campbell. He leaves for Taupo on Monday."

Wellington

WE WENT FROM Port Lyttelton by steamer to Wellington, passing on our way northwards the Kaikora [Kaikoura] mountains, which make the coast of the province of Marlborough magnificent. They are snow-clad, and of beautiful form, and to a member of the Alpine Club, would offer, I should think, irresistible temptation. The town of Wellington, now the capital of the colony, stands high up in a bay which was originally called Port Nicholson. The site as seen from the sea is very lovely, as the town is surrounded by hills, and is open only to the water. It reminded me much of St Thomas, —among the Virgin Islands; but in appearance only. St Thomas is one of the most unhealthy places frequented by man, whereas there is perhaps no spot more healthy than Wellington. It is however, noted for being windy, and the character seems to be deserved. The town is built only of wood, including even the Parliament House, which is a very spacious building, and the Government House, which is a handsome English mansion.

From the position in which Wellington stands, and the manner in which it is surrounded by the sea on all sides but one, it is too closely hemmed in, and too destitute of land immediately around it, for extensive prosperity as a town. It contains something under 8,000 inhabitants, whereas the population both of the city of Auckland and Dunedin, with their suburbs, is over 20,000 each, and that of Christchurch is over 12,000.[1] But it is a pleasant little town, and when the

---

1. Nearly a century later (1966 census) the population of New Zealand's four main cities had increased to: Auckland 565,500; Wellington 170,500; Christchurch 252,900; Dunedin 109,400.

North Island of New Zealand, showing places mentioned by Trollope.

General Assembly is sitting it is gay enough. Of course, it is subject to the condition of all cities which have been chosen as capitals, not on account of their commercial prosperity, but because they are centrally situated for political purposes. Wellington is a very poor place when Congress is not there, and I imagine that life at Ottawa must be also when the representatives of the people are away from it.

There are interesting spots around Wellington. Within two or three miles of the town there are the remains of a New Zealand forest,—than which no forest is more lovely. They are absolutely impervious, unless a way be cut through them, owing to the thick growth of the forest vines. They are green throughout the year,—not with a dull, greyish-green tint, such as that of the Australian gum,—but are bright with semi-tropical growth. The hills all round the town were a few years since covered with such forests, but there is now but little left of them. A botanical garden is in course of construction, which has great advantages in the lie of the lands, and the shape of the surrounding hills. It is a pity perhaps that it was not commenced before so much of the surrounding timber was taken away.

I visited the valley of the Hutt, so named after that old coloniser, the present member for Gateshead[1], up which one of the new railways is being formed,—with, I should think, questionable political economy as there is water carriage from Wellington up to the Hutt, and there may well be doubts whether the pastoral districts in the valleys beyond will afford traffic sufficient to pay for working the line.[2] But it is the policy of New Zealand to spend money, and to look for that prosperity which is supposed to come from a generous expenditure. And

---

1. Sir William Hutt (1801-1882). A founder of the New Zealand Company.
2. The Hutt valley is on the route of the railway to Napier and Gisborne on the east coast.

I was taken up to the Horokiwi valley, a beautiful glen, some forty miles out of the town. From the head of the valley, on the coach road from Wellington to Wanganui and Taranaki, the traveller rises on to a range of hills from whence he looks down on the eastern coast[1] and the river, and the island of Kapiti. The view here is very fine, and at the same time very interesting to those who concern themselves closely in the history of New Zealand and her troubles; for here it was that the great chief Rauparaha lived, and near to this spot, at Porirua, he was taken prisoner, not in warfare, but by stratagem. . . . I had the pleasure of meeting his son[2] at the Governor's table, and of playing battledore and shuttlecock with him in the Governor's hall. For this Rauparaha is also a great man among the Maoris, and is very friendly with the white men. It is said of him, the present man, that he has killed men, but never eaten them; of his father, that he had killed and eaten men,—and he had no doubt eaten a great many; but of his grandfather, that he had killed men and eaten them, and had then himself been killed and eaten, like a true old Maori warrior as he was.

At Horokiwi we dined and slept, and the Governor,[3] whose guests we were, asked an old chieftain who was coming along the coast to dine with us. He was tattooed all over up to his

---

1. Horokiwi looks down on the west, not the east coast.
2. Tamihana Te Rauparaha (1819-1876). The younger son of the notorious chief Te Rauparaha. The Dictionary of New Zealand Biography describes him as "a young man of singular strength of character and steadfastness of purpose." He became an early convert to Christianity, and in 1843, with a companion, Matene, he ministered, at the risk of his life, to his father's enemies at Banks Peninsula and Kaiapoi. In 1852 he visited England with Bishop Williams and was presented to Queen Victoria. He was a prime mover in the proposal for uniting the tribes under a Maori king.
3. Sir George Bowen (1821-1899), Governor of New Zealand in succession to Sir George Grey, 1867-1873.

hair, and round almost up to the nape of his neck,—and he wore a great chimney-pot about 15 inches high, as some men used to wear in London a quarter of a century ago. He was very careful with his hat, and ate his dinner solemnly, with excellent appetite. When asked his opinion about this and that other Maori chief, he shook his head in disgust. They were all bad men, and had had too much land awarded to them. He rode a wretched old horse, and said that he was going about for pleasure to spend a month among his friends.

It must, I think, be conceded in reference to new countries, such as are our Australian colonies and New Zealand, that it would not only be impossible that they should develop their resources without borrowing money on the security of the wealth to be produced,—but also that it would be unjust to the present generation to make the attempt, were it thought possible that that success should be so achieved. In an old country, such as our own,—the government is not called upon to develop its resources: I will take railroads as an illustration of what I mean when I speak of the resources of a country. Railroads with us have been made by private companies, the members of which have considered that they saw the means of turning their capital to good account in such enterprises. Whether they have been right or wrong in so considering, the capital and the spirit to spend it have been sufficient, and the railways have been made. But in the colonies such a state of things is out of the question. The capital does not exist, and the fact is patent to all men that the railroads when made would not pay a fair interest,—very often that they would pay no interest whatsoever,—on the money to be expended on their construction.

It is equally patent that nothing tends so quickly to enrich a country and to enable a people to use the wealth which God has placed within their reach, as a ready conveyance for themselves and their goods. Wheat is not grown, because it cannot be conveyed to market. Copper and coal and iron are left unworked, because they cannot be profitably conveyed away. Wool-growers dare hardly venture to distant pastures, awed by the same difficulty. The young colony therefore demands a railroad,—which the government only can make, and can do so only by the means which its parliament shall grant to it. Then arises the question whether the present or a future generation shall pay for the railroad,—and it becomes at once apparent to the shallowest thinker that, even were it possible to saddle the country with immediate taxation sufficient for the purpose, it would be most unjust to do so. Why should we, who are struggling here today, make a railroad for the benefit of those who are to come after us, and who in all human probability will be much better able than we are to bear the expense? This same argument applies to roads, harbours, bridges, public buildings, and all institutions as to which the public will possess the completed property. Therefore the money is borrowed, and the present generation feels that it bears its fair share of the burden by paying the interest as it accrues.

The argument is good, and the practice will probably have the adherence of all sagacious statesmen, as long as the value of the property actually created by the expenditure does not sink below the amount of the debt incurred. As long as such a state of things is preserved, the colony or country cannot in truth be said to be in debt at all. Its assets are equal to its liabilities, and its annual revenue in such a condition will infallibly preserve it from any inconvenient pressure upon its means. The colony of Victoria now owes a debt of twelve millions, but very nearly the whole of this sum has been expended in railways, and the remainder on works of similar permanent value,—and Victoria is in truth not indebted. That unfortunately is not the case with New Zealand. Her wars with the Maoris, which have been declared by competent authority at home to have cost England twelve millions, have cost that colony nearly four millions and a half.

And again, in considering the matter of borrowing for public works it must be remembered that, unfortunately, inducements other than those of the direct public good may induce ministers to ask for loans, and may allure members of parliament to grant them. Or even if the motives of ministers and of members be as pure as Patriotism herself, there may be lacking the sagacity necessary for the profitable expenditure of public funds. Or, as is much more commonly the case, the motives, and the sagacity also, may be mixed. A minister may assure himself that his sole object is his country's good, and that he is spending himself night and day on her behalf, that he is remunerated, by a clerk's beggarly salary, for energies and intellect which would make a fortune for him if devoted to trade; and in this way he may be as sure of his own virtue as were Pitt and Peel. But not the less does he teach himself to think that the one thing most necessary for his country's welfare is his own continuance in office, and to effect that,—simply for his country's good, and to his own personal ruin,—he will make compromises with dishonesty, or perhaps rush into a policy of which the only value to his country will consist in the fact that it will obtain for himself a popularity among voters outside sufficient to keep him in office.

When a minister achieves the power of handling millions in the manufacture of railways, the temptation to waste hundreds of thousands is very heavy on him. Each portion of a colony, each district, or each province, wants its railway. "A railway for you gentlemen down south!" says a northern member. "Certainly,—but on condition that we have one here, up north!" To an eager politician, anxious to please his own constituency, it matters little that it be shown to him that there will be little for the northern railway to carry, while the other may be expected to do a fair business. Votes are counted, and the northern gentlemen has his way. Then, again, it comes to pass that a large part of the population in a new country finds so great a benefit from the immediate expenditure of the money,—labourers who get the government wages, and of course vote, and tradesmen who cater for the labourers, and of course vote,—that the patriotic minister, anxious only for his country's good, finds that the country will certainly be robbed of his services unless he maintain this popular condition of things. In such circumstances a minister is apt,—I will not say to become unscrupulous,—but to allow a great latitude to his scruples.

And then there is also the danger,—from which nations, as well as colonies, have suffered,—of there arising some Cagliostro in politics, some conjuror in statecraft, who shall be clever enough to talk steady men off their legs by fine phrases, and to dazzle the world around him by new inventions in the management of affairs. Such men can invest democratic measures with tendencies purely conservative, can run into debt upon theories of the strictest economy, and commingle patriotic principles with cosmopolitan practices in a manner very charming to weak minds. A statesman of this class is of necessity unscrupulous, and to a young community may be ruinous. It is his hope to leap to great success by untried experiments,—and being willing himself to run the risk of extermination if he fail, he does not hesitate to bind his country to his own chariot wheels as he rushes into infinite space. Such a minister in a colony, should he get the power of the purse into his hands, will throw his millions about without any reference to the value of the property acquired. He will learn the charm of spending with profusion, and will almost teach himself to measure the prosperity of the community which is subject to him, by the amount which it owes.

When I reached Wellington, a vote of want of confidence in the present ministry had just been brought before the

House of Representatives by Mr Stafford[1], so that I had the opportunity of hearing a debate in which the ministry and their opponents were fighting for possession of immediate political power. The same thing had occurred when I was at Sydney, and there the minister had been forced to resign. . . . I had been present at a similar battle in Melbourne, in which the minister was defeated, there also,—and had been driven to resign, after a terrible conflict, at the close of which the Governor refused to him the privilege of dissolving the House, for which he had pleaded. These facts doubtless affected the conditions of the combat in New Zealand. It was felt that the Governor would not dissolve the House, and that the ministers, if beaten, would not risk the chance of a refusal. There was therefore no immediate means of effacing their defeat within their reach, should they be beaten by the vote then to be given; and the fight was therefore signally one of life and death. . . . When I reached the capital general opinion gave the ministers a majority of three or four. As days passed by this imagined superiority dwindled to a supposed tie. On the morning of the day on which the division was taken it was believed that there would be one against them. On that night they were beaten by a majority of two.

Three adverse resolutions were proposed to the House, but, as is usual in such cases, they who attacked the ministers assailed their entire policy. It did not require a long sojourn in the colony to enable an observer to understand that distrust of Mr Vogel was the feeling which first made the attack possible and then rendered it successful. Mr Fox[2] was Premier, but I think

---

1. Edward William (later Sir E. W.) Stafford (1819-1901). Prime Minister 1856, 1865 and 1872.
2. William (later Sir William) Fox (1812-1893). Prime Minister 1856, 1861, 1869, 1873. Author. Painter. Climbed Mount Egmont at age of 80. Founder of the New Zealand [Temperance] Alliance. Knighted 1879.

that I shall not be held by that gentleman to do injustice to his position as a minister, if I say that Mr Vogel was regarded by the colony as the acting spirit of the cabinet. Mr Fox held no portfolio, whereas Mr Vogel was, as we say, Chancellor of the Exchequer, or Colonial Treasurer as he is called at the Antipodes. Now New Zealand had latterly been pre-eminently conspicuous for spending money,—and conspicuous also for the amount of money which she intended to spend. It had seemed to be Mr Vogel's theory of government that blood should be infused into the veins of a young community, and energy given to the action of the heart, by an open-handed, and I may perhaps say, profuse liberality. Railways were to be created throughout the colony. Railways in Auckland, railways in Wellington, railways as I have before said even in Marlborough, railways from the southern point of the Middle Island through Otago and Canterbury, up to Nelson were to leave no district in the colony unsatisfied. And the natives were to be kept quiet by a good-humoured liberality, which would leave them nothing to gain by rebellion.

That a colony should have life in it all New Zealanders were willing to allow,—for they are an energetic people. And they were ready to admit that public credit is too grand a thing not to be used for raising this life,—for they are a sanguine people. Mr Vogel's theory had had its charms for them, as is proved with sufficient clearness by the money which he has borrowed. But that which at first was taken for dash and good courage, seemed to many after a while to become recklessness and fool-hardihood. Mr Vogel was playing a great experiment, at the expense of the community, and the colony began to ask who was Mr Vogel, that it should trust him? I am constrained to

say, looking back at the figures on the previous page, that I
think the colony trusted him too far.[1]

The old ministry was beaten, and a new ministry came in.
But when I left New Zealand it was held to be doubtful
whether the new ministry could stand, and since I have returned
home Mr Vogel has been restored to his seat on the Treasury
Bench. A majority of two for purpose of defeat does not give
assurance of a working majority,—and it was said at once that
there were dissensions. As I have given my own opinion of
Mr Vogel as a minister, I am bound to say that many men
in the colony believe in him,—that they think that a new

---

1. In 1875 Trollope visited Australia for a second time, and
touched at Auckland on the way home.

There is, in the Bett collection at the Alexander Turnbull
Library, Wellington, a letter of Sir William Fox to an unknown
correspondent, dated at Manchester, 19th November 1875, in
the course of which he refers to Trollope:

" Mr A. Trollope writing from San Francisco on his return
from Australia and after 6 hours stay in Auckland has published
one of his letters in several English papers (I saw it in the
Northern Echo) running down Vogel, and predicting the ruin
and bankruptcy of N.Zd. on acct. of reckless borrowing etc. It
is a disgraceful production. No one seems to have thought it
their business in London to reply to it, and though I would have
done so myself, I have been prevented by not having access to
public documents at a distance from London."

It is an interesting circumstance that Trollope, Vogel and
Fox appear to have been in England at about the same time. ·

Referring to the period following Trollope's 1872 visit, Dr
Scholefield (*Dictionary of New Zealand Biography*) had this
to say: 'The Vogel policy was now in full swing. Railways
were creeping forward in all parts of the country;" and he
refers to Vogel's " dazzling record of achievement." Trollope's
prophecy of disaster was, of course, never near. Nevertheless the
borrowing policy was followed, a few years later, by a temporary
period of depression, the intensity of which, says Scholefield
"was undoubtedly increased by the reckless pace at which Vogel
had moved in the seventies."

prophet has arisen, whom absence of timidity will enable him to manage politics as they have never been managed before, and who will create prosperity out of expenditure. Mr Vogel is now again in a position to throw his money broadcast over the land, and it may be that he will continue to do so,— while the credit of the colony lasts.[1]

I was often asked in New Zealand whether the line of parliamentary debate in that colony did not contrast favourably with that which I had heard in the Australian parliaments. I am bound to say that at Wellington I heard no word to which any Speaker of a House could take exception, and that this propriety of language was maintained while very hard things were being said by members one of another. This is, I think, as it should be. The life necessary for political debate cannot be maintained without the saying of hard things; but the use of hard words makes debate at first unbearable, and after a time impracticable. But I thought that the method of talking practised in the New Zealand House of Representatives was open to censure on another head. I have never in any national debating assembly,—not even at Washington,— seen so constant a reference to papers on the part of those who were speaking as was made in this debate. It seemed as though barrows full of papers must have been brought in for the use of gentlemen on one side or on the other. From this arises the great evil of slowness. The gentleman on his legs in the House, —when custom has made that position easy to him,—learns to take delight in delaying the House while he turns over one folio after another either of manuscript, which has been arranged for him, or of printed matter which he has marked

---

1. The ministry of Sir Julius Vogel substantially lasted until 1877, though Vogel was temporarily absent in England in 1875, and in 1876 was appointed New Zealand's Agent-General in London. In 1877 a new ministry came into office, with Sir George Grey as Premier.

for reference. And then, to show how very much at home he is, while gentlemen are gaping around him, he will look out for new references, muttering perhaps a word or two while his face is among the leaves,—perhaps repeating the last words of his last sentence, and absolutely revelling in the tyranny of his position. But while doing so, he is unconsciously losing the orator's power of persuasion. I doubt whether Demosthenes often looked at his papers, or Cicero when he was speaking, or Pitt. Judging from what I have seen from the strangers' gallery at home, I should say that a New Zealand minister had learned to carry to an absurdity a practice which is authorised, and no more than authorised, by the usage of our House of Commons. A Speaker, on observing such fault, can hardly call the offender to order,—but he might have the power of putting out the gas.

I cannot conclude my remarks about the Wellington Assembly and the debate which I heard there, without saying that the four Maori members discreetly spread their votes, two supporting and two voting against, the ministry.

Mr Anthony Trollope in Wellington

AN INTERVIEW WITH ANTHONY TROLLOPE

A short paragraph in the *Evening Star* (Dunedin) of the 26th September, 1872, stated: "The literary 'Jeames' who acts as the Wellington correspondent of the *Southern Cross* lately forwarded that journal a minute description of Mr Anthony Trollope, even to his spectacles." That report appeared in the *Wellington Independent* of the 17th September:

A correspondent of the *Southern Cross* (we understand Mr Luckie, M.H.R.) writes as follows: "A visit to Wellington from a great author, son of a great writer, has given a little zest to current events among those who take interest in great personages who have made themselves so by the possession and exercise of brains, taste, judgment, and above all, knowledge of mankind. The last is the true accompaniment of genius, because it fixes the colouring of a present time in marvellous fictions such as those which our great authors have handed down from their own days to ours, and to those of future generations. . . . I don't desire to get sentimental, or write a Young Men's Mutual Improvement Association essay, because I happen to have to announce the fact that Anthony Trollope, the novelist, the son of a celebrated literary author, is now in Wellington. He arrived in the Alhambra, and purposes visiting Auckland and surroundings in a few weeks.

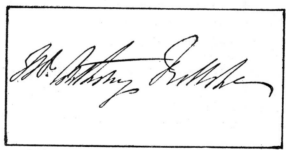

Visiting card. (Original in Alexander Turnbull Library, Wellington.)

"Shall I try to describe him? He is tall, squarely built, slightly florid faced, portly in figure, yet singularly light in his step, and with a buoyancy and springiness reminding one of the free and elastic gait of Bishop Selwyn. A bright hazel eye looks at his interlocuter through spectacles, and a pleasant decided kind of voice is suggestive of being that of a man who has seen for himself, taken in all surrounding circumstances, weighed them, compared them, and drawn his conclusions according to the evidence.

"It is surprising how in half-an-hour's conversation you can discover how much he knows of the state of affairs. I mean social affairs in New Zealand—those things that affect and more or less completely guide and dominate the circumstances and condition of people. He knows the pictures and interiors of middle-class life here, and status and pay of people's servants.

when they have any, the price of labour, the condition of the
working man, the cost of living, the rate of rents, the general
condition and well-being of the mass of people as exhibited by
what he has seen during his brief but most observant journeyings.
He has been to the Assembly, and heard, amongst others, Mr
Vogel's speech on the no confidence debate; and I happen to
know that of that speech Mr Trollope spoke in terms of high
praise, and that it would have befitted and been listened to in
the atmosphere of St Stephen's. . . . Of course he did not put
it in those words, for he is averse to periphrastic or pedantic
utterances. . . . He and Mrs Trollope are living at Government
House, and I hear he purposes taking a long ride through
different parts of the country if the departure of the San
Francisco mail in October will permit him. Someone acquainted
with the country should be sent as a guide to take him to the
Hot Springs, to Lake Taupo, Rotorua, &c.

"Mr Anthony Trollope is the youngest of the two literary
sons of a literary mother. He held for a number of years a
responsible position in the Post Office under the late Sir
Rowland Hill, after whose death he resigned and contested a
seat for Parliament (Heverley) in the Liberal interest; but
through some corruption on the part of his opponent's agents,
the seat, on a petition brought by Mr Trollope's friends, was
declared still vacant, and a new writ was issued; Mr Trollope,
however, declined again to contest the election, having seen too
much of the hollowness of politics; and it is well that he did
so, for future generations will gain more from Anthony Trollope,
the novelist, the beholder of the life of humanity in all quarters
of the world, and the skilful inter-weaver of the woof of
fancy and fiction with the weft of fact, as witnessed by himself,
than from Trollope, the politician, one of 666 M.P's. He is a
member of a greater and far more select guild, the guild of
high literature. . . .

Mr Trollope was born in 1815; was educated at Winchester
and Harrow. His novels, the first of which was published in
1847, are numerous, and I observe that, since his arrival here,
every one of the series has been taken out of the Assembly
Library, so anxious are people to be "up" in the writings of
the present hero of the hour. . . . Here is a list of the novels,
and people who have not time to read or re-read them, and

yet desire to look learned by referring to the name, can do so from this list, for a knowledge of indices is very often liable to be taken for a profundity of reading, especially as most of your hearers are afraid to enter into particulars lest they should disclose their own ignorance. This seems sarcastic, but I am in excellent humour, and it is, I think, very true. . . ."

There follows a list of Trollope's novels up to that period, and a biographical sketch of Anthony's brother Adolphus.

D. M. Luckie (1828-1909) was a Scottish journalist who, arriving in New Zealand in 1863, became part-proprietor and editor of the *Nelson Colonist*. From 1869 to 1872, he represented Nelson in the Provincial Council, and from 1873, represented Nelson City in Parliament. In 1876, when the *Southern Cross* amalgamated with the *New Zealand Herald*, Luckie was appointed editor, and later became editor of the *Evening Post*, Wellington. In 1894 he published *The Raid of the Russian Cruiser Kaskowiski*, to impress upon the New Zealand public the danger of being unprepared for possible invasion.

Taranaki

(Mr and Mrs Trollope took the west coast route from Wellington to Onehunga, travelling by way of Picton, Nelson and New Plymouth, where they appear to have attracted no attention by the press.)

B Y THE CONSTITUTION of 1852 New Zealand was divided into six provinces, of which New Plymouth was the smallest in area, in white population, and in the amount of land purchased from the natives by the Europeans; but in native population it ranked next to Auckland and Wellington, and among all the native tribes there were perhaps none so hostile to the settlers as those of Taranaki. In 1858 the province of New Plymouth assumed, by Act of the General Assembly, the old native name of Taranaki, keeping the English appellation for its capital. In 1853 the native population of the province was estimated at 3,000, and the Europeans were estimated to be 1,985. In 1871 the Europeans had increased to 4,480, having something more than doubled themselves. In the province of Auckland they had increased sixfold; in that of Wellington, including Hawke Bay,—a new province formed out of Wellington,—they had increased more than fourfold, in that of Nelson, including Marlborough, formed out of it,—nearly sixfold; in that of Canterbury,—including the county of Westland, formed out of it,—nearly sixteenfold; and in that of Otago twentyfold. In the meantime the Maori population had certainly decreased in every province except that of Taranaki, —in which, owing to the shifting of the tribes in consequence of the wars, it has not improbably increased. As by far the greater portion of the province is not at present accessible to Europeans, as we have no settlements in those districts, occupy

103

no land, and as, in fact, the Queen's law does not run there, no information can be obtained with any precision as to the number of natives there located. The figures above given are sufficient to show that of all parts of New Zealand, this has been the least progressive, and that, in the improbable event of a further Maori war, property here would be more precarious than elsewhere.

I was informed at New Plymouth,—during the five hours that I stayed there,—that the settlers are presumed to own about 150,000 acres, claiming to have bought that amount from the natives; that of this about 80,000 acres were in the possession of persons preparing to occupy them,—that is, ready to go on their property when things should be sufficiently settled to enable them to do so,—but that no more than 22,000 acres were actually at present in permanent use. I find that in 1870 no acre of country land,—as distinct from urban and suburban land,—was bought by the settlers at Taranaki, though in that year land in all the other provinces, was either bought, or given to immigrants, or made over to military settlers. Wool-growing is the trade of the Middle Island rather than of the Northern; but from every other province in both the islands rent is received by the government for pastures. But no such rent is received by the government from Taranaki.

And yet when the New Zealand Land Company planted a young community of settlers here in 1841, New Plymouth was called the garden of New Zealand. The land is said to be good, but light. Hitherto the people have not grown wheat enough for their own consumption. The little town is beautifully situated under Mount Egmont, which is 10,000 feet high,[1]— with a lovely summit of snow, sharp almost as a church steeple. The land around Mount Egmont is grandly timbered, and said to be of high quality; but, at thirty miles distant from the

---

1. The height is 8,260 feet.

town, it is held by the natives, and is inaccessible. And then there is no harbour at New Plymouth,—a want which must go far to mar the prosperity of the settlement.[1]

All along this coast the sand is composed chiefly of iron, or, as the people there say, of steel,—so that when you handle it, though it be as soft as sand, it is almost as heavy as iron. I was told that from some of it 70 percent of pure metal has been extracted. Works have been established at New Plymouth for uplifting the iron, and making steel,—but have never as yet prospered, from the want of a proper flux for the metal.[2] I heard the matter discussed there, at Auckland, and elsewhere, and the opinion seemed general that ultimately these sands would become the source of great wealth. They are found along the east[3] shore of the North Island as far as Manukau Harbour, in the province of Auckland. The sensation of weight when the soft stuff is gathered in the hand is very remarkable.

"I do not quite see," said I, to one of the leaders among the citizens who was kindly showing me the place, "how ordinary trade can hold its head up in a place so small and so remote." "It does," said he, "and we never have any bankrupts." I could not continue my ill-nature by remarking that there can be no bankruptcy without credit.

But there is the province, with its own little House of Commons, with its own Superintendent, and its own three members in the General Assembly at Wellington; and if it lives,—as it surely now will live,—till the Maories [Maoris] have melted[4], it will have scope for its energies, and land in which to grow its own corn.

---

1. The whole of Taranaki is now in production, and a breakwater provides good shelter for large vessels.
2. Steps are now (1969) being taken to test the economic potential of Taranaki ironsand.
3. The west shore.
4. See previous notes concerning the resurgence of the Maori population.

Auckland

AUCKLAND still considers herself to be, and certainly has been, the leading province of New Zealand. In the old days, before the colony had been divided into provinces,—before the colony was a colony,—the northern portion of the Northern Island was the only part of New Zealand with which Europeans were acquainted. It was here that the Pakeha-Maoris[1] settled themselves and dwelt with the natives. It was here that Governor Hobson fixed the seat of the government. It was here,—up at Kororareka,—that Heke cut down the flagstaff. It was here that Bishop Selwyn was settled when there was only one bishop in New Zealand, and it was here that all the governors have lived[2], and here the general parliament was held, till the seat of government was moved to Wellington in 1864. The province of Otago is now the most populous of the provinces, and its capital, Dunedin, the most populous of New Zealand cities[3]. And as Otago is also the most southern province, and is therefore far removed from Auckland; and as Canterbury, also in the south, has grown in power and population; there came to be the same feeling in regard to Auckland that existed in Canada respecting Quebec,—and therefore the capital was removed to the central, but comparatively small town of Wellington.

---

1. Pakeha-Maori was a term applied to traders and others of the pre-settlement era.
2. There is still a Government House at Auckland, but the Governor-General usually resides at Government House, Wellington.
3. See previous note concerning Dunedin, which is now New Zealand's fourth city in respect of population.

Because of its age, and old history, and early dealings with the Maoris, I regard Auckland as being the representative city of New Zealand. . . . Dunedin, which hardly knows the appearance of a Maori as well as does London, where the interesting stranger has been seen at Exeter Hall, has no title to be considered. Dunedin is a Scotch town and Christchurch an English town, here planted,—and Auckland is redolent of New Zealand. Her streets are still traversed by Maoris and half-castes, and the Pakeha-Maori still wanders into town from his distant settlement in quest of tea, sugar and brandy.

And the councils by which New Zealand has been governed as a colony in the perilous days which she has passed, were all held at Auckland. It was here that over and over again peace with the natives has been decided upon as the policy of the day, till peace was no longer possible and the colony drifted into war. Though both parties desired peace,—and such I believe was the desire of each party,—peace was impossible because they did not desire it on the same basis. "Peace, certainly,—but of course we must hold our own," said the white man. The Maori said identically the same thing,—but the possession claimed as "our own" was one and the same, namely, the right to decide questions of property, each according to his own laws. It may be imagined that at Auckland there is a feeling that Dunedin and Christchurch are interlopers, as New Zealand towns. The Maori war has been the great feature of the colony of New Zealand, and Otago and Canterbury have had no more to do with the war than Buckinghamshire and Berkshire. Therefore Auckland still considers herself to be the capital of the colony,—and it has much reason in its claim.

It may be well to notice here the fact that as Auckland considers herself to be the cream of New Zealand, so does New Zealand consider herself to be the cream of the British empire. The pretension is made in, I think, every British

colony that I visited. I remember that it was insisted upon
with absolute confidence in Barbadoes; that no Demeraran
doubted it in British Guiana; that it was hinted at in Jamaica
with as much energy as was left for any opinion in that
unhappy island; and that in Bermuda a confidence in potatoes,
onions and oleanders, had produced the same effect. In Canada
the conviction is so rife that a visitor hardly cares to dispute
it. In New South Wales it crops out even in those soft
murmurings with which men there regret their mother country.
In Queensland the assertion is always supported by a reference
to the doubtful charms of her perhaps too luxurious climate.
In Victoria the boast is made with true Yankee confidence in
"our institutions." Victoria declares herself to be different from
England, and therefore better.

But in New Zealand the assurance is altogether of a different
nature. The New Zealander among John Bulls is the most
John-Bullish. He admits the supremacy of England to every
place in the world, only he is more English than any Englishman
at home. He tells you that he has the same climate,—only
somewhat improved; that he grows the same produce,—only
with somewhat heavier crops; that he has the same beautiful
scenery at his doors,—only somewhat grander in its nature
and more diversified in its details; that he follows the same
pursuits and after the same fashion,—but with less of misery,
less of want, and more general participation in the gifts which
God has given to the country. He reminds you that at Otago,
in the south, the mean temperature is the same as at London,
whereas at Auckland, in the north, he has just that improvement
necessary to furnish the most perfect climate in the world.
The mean temperature of the coldest month in London is
37deg, which is only five degrees above freezing, whereas
at Auckland it is 51deg, which enables growth to continue
throughout the whole year. Of the hottest month the mean
temperature at Auckland is only 68deg, which,—says the

Aucklander,—neither hinders a European from working, nor debilitates his constitution. All good things have been given to this happy land and, when the Maori has melted, here will be the navel of the earth. I know nothing to allege against the assurance. It is a land very happy in its climate;—very happy in its promises. The poor Maori who is now the source of all Auckland poetry, must first melt[1]; and then, if her coal-fields can be made productive,—for she has coal-fields,—and the iron which is washed to her shore among the sands of the sea, can be wrought into steel, I see no reason why Auckland should not rival London. I must specially observe one point as to which the New Zealand colonist imitates his brethren and ancestors at home;—and far surpasses his Australian rival. He is very fond of getting drunk. And I would also observe to the New Zealander generally, as I have done to other colonists, that if he would blow his trumpet somewhat less loudly, the music would gain in its effect upon the world at large. . . .

As I had seen many gold-fields in Australia, and gone down many mines—to the great disturbance of my peace and happiness,—and had generally gone away with the impression that I had learned but little by my personal inspection, I did not visit the Thames gold-fields. I am, however, able to say, from enquiry on the subject, that the miners as a body conduct themselves with that general courtesy of manners which I found to be universal among the Australian mining population. I own that I had thought before visiting the colonies that contact with gold made men rough. I am bound to say that, as regards the workers themselves, it seems to have the opposite effect.

Kauri gum—an article of trade found, as far as I am aware, only in the province of Auckland,—has been of material service

---

1. The Maori, who stood shoulder to shoulder with the Pakeha in two world wars, shows a determination not to "melt!"

to the colony. It is used in the glazing of calico, and as a cheap substitute for copal varnish in the preparation of furniture; and also,—if the assertion be not calumny, for the manufacture of amber mouthpieces[1]. I chipped a morsel of kauri gum one day with my penknife in a merchant's store, and then chipped the mouthpiece of my tobacco pipe. The chipping seemed to be identical. I don't see why kauri gum should not make very good mouthpieces for pipes; but if so, the consumer ought to have the advantage. Kauri gum, at the wholesale price, is worth from 30s to 40s per cwt; and as it is very light, a great many pipes could be made beautiful with a hundredweight of kauri gum. In 1870 the amount exported fetched £175,074; and in 1871, £167,958.

The kauri gum exudes from the kauri tree, but is not got by any process of tapping, or by taking the gum from the tree while standing. The tree falls and dies, as trees do fall and die in the course of nature;—whole forests fall and die; and then when the timber has rotted away, when centuries probably have passed, the gum is found beneath the soil. Practice tells the kauri gum seekers where to search for the hidden spoil. Armed with a long spear, the man prods the earth;—and from the touch he knows the gum when he strikes it. Hundreds of thousands of tons probably still lie buried beneath the soil; but the time will come when the kauri gum will be at an end, for the forests are falling now, not by the slow and kind operation of nature, but beneath the rapid axes of the settlers.

I was taken out of Auckland by a friend to see a kauri forest. Very shortly there will be none to be seen[2] unless the

---

1. Kauri gum, in general, is too brittle to be suitable for mouth-pieces, ingenious as may be the suggestion. The kauri gum industry is now practically extinct. During the century 1850-1950 gum to the value of about £25,000,000 was exported.

2. The kauri forest seen by Trollope is still in existence. Early in the 20th century a large area of the Waitakere ranges, a few

(See next page.)

searcher for it goes very far afield. I was well repaid for my trouble, for I doubt whether I ever saw finer trees grouped together, and yet the foliage of them is neither graceful nor luxuriant. It is scanty, and grows in tufts like little bushes. But the trunks of the trees, and the colour of the timber, and the form of the branches are magnificent. The chief peculiarity seems to be that the trunk appears not to lessen in size at all till it throws out its branches at twenty-five or perhaps thirty feet from the ground, and looks therefore like a huge forest column. We saw one, to which we were taken by a woodman whom we found at his work, the diameter of which was nine feet, and of which we computed the height up to the first branches to be fifty feet. And the branches are almost more than large in proportion to the height, spreading out after the fashion of an oak,—only in greater proportions.

These trees are fast disappearing. Our friend the woodman told us that the one to which he took us,—and than which he assured us that we could find none larger in the forest,—was soon to fall beneath his axe. When we met him he was triumphing over a huge monster that he had felled, and was splitting it up into shingles for roofing houses. The wood as it comes to pieces is yellow and resinous with gum, and on that account,—so he told us,—was super-excellent for shingles. The trees are never cut down for their gum, which seems to be useless till time has given it a certain consistency[1]. Very soon there will not be a kauri tree left to cut down in the neighbourhood of Auckland.

---

miles west of Auckland city, was set aside as a scenic reserve. The largest officially measured kauri was 66 feet in girth and 100 feet in height to the first limb. There is reliable evidence for a tree with a girth of 72 feet. Other large areas of kauri forest have been reserved, and much re-afforestation of this world-famous timber tree is being undertaken.

1. At a somewhat later period, gum oozing from the trunk and branches was also collected and exported.

Many of us still remember the kind of halo which surrounded Bishop Selwyn when he first came out to New Zealand. . . . This arose partly from his reputation, partly from his being much loved by many good men, partly, no doubt, from the fact that his episcopate was an experiment among a more than usually savage race of savages,—who also, as savages, were more than usually powerful and intelligent. Bishops who went to Calcutta and Sydney were sent out simply to guide the Churches of England established for the use of exiles from our own shores. They certainly did not go out as missionaries. . . . But the Bishop of New Zealand went out, not only to guide the Church of England on behalf of the colonists, but also to Christianise the Maori. There can be no question of the zeal, the intellect, and the sagacity with which he did his work[1].

When at Auckland I had the pleasure of meeting Sir George Grey[2], whose name has been so intimately connected with the fortunes of New Zealand, whether in peace or war. He is now residing at the island of Kawau, some miles from the harbour, and is there turning a wilderness into a garden. I have endeavoured in my remarks about the colonies to abstain from offering opinions as to the conduct of governors who are still living. From many I have received kind hospitality, and I think that a writer for the public should not praise when he feels himself to be deterred by friendship from censure. But, as to Sir George Grey, I may fairly say, without expressing any opinion of my own as to his conduct as governor, that he certainly managed to endear himself in a wonderful way to a population with whom it was his duty to be constantly

---

1. Anglican, Methodist and Roman Catholic missionaries had of course been labouring among the Maoris for a number of years before the arrival of Bishop Selwyn.

2. Sir George Grey (1812-1901). At the time of Trollope's visit Grey had temporarily retired, but later entered politics.

fighting. There can be no doubt of Sir George Grey's popularity among the Maoris.

The harbour of Auckland is very pretty,—though hardly so picturesque as those of Lyttelton or Wellington;—and it is trustworthy for ships. The immediate harbour is landlocked by the island called Rangitoto, and the bay beyond, called Hauraki Gulf, is again guarded by two further islands, called the Great and Little Barrier. Its ports have been the making of Auckland, which stands on so narrow a neck of land, that it has another harbour called the Manukau, within seven miles of the city on the western coast.—Auckland itself being on the eastern. This double seaboard has given the place a great advantage, as a portion of the intercolonial trade is made by the eastern route. Thence is made the quickest route to Wellington, Nelson, and Hokitika, and to Melbourne;—and by this route the passengers from Otago and Christchurch generally reach the north. But the direct course from Auckland out to the world at large, is by Rangitoto and the Barriers. Till within the last few years, the direct course from Great Britain to New Zealand was round the Cape of Good Hope or by the isthmus of Suez and the Australian colonies;—and the direct route home was by Cape Horn or back by Suez; but now a line of American steamers has been established direct from San Francisco to Auckland, which carries the mails under a contract with the New Zealand government, and which will be a popular route for passengers as soon as a certain prejudice is overcome which in British minds is apt to attach itself to American enterprises.

The scenery of the Middle Island, though perhaps as fine as anything in Europe, is, I think, altogether unknown, even by character, to English travellers. At any rate, I heard little or nothing of it till I was on my way to New Zealand, and was preparing myself by enquiry for the journey. But I had heard much of geysers or hot springs of the province of

Auckland, and was aware that I could see in the North Island jets of boiling water and of steam,—such as could be found elsewhere only in Iceland. One of my first anxieties was to be put in the way of making an excursion into the hot-water territory in such a fashion that I might see whatever was worth seeing,—and this, through the kindness of the Governor, I was able to accomplish.

It must be understood that at present there is no road into this country[1], which lies south of the city of Auckland,—or I may perhaps more accurately say south of the Bay of Plenty, which forms a considerable bight in the very irregular north-western [north-eastern] coast-line. There is at present no completed road, but roads to it are being made in three directions. There is the route north from Napier, the capital of Hawke [Hawkes] Bay, by which a coach runs,—with a short intermediate space of ten miles, over which passengers were still carried on horseback in September, 1872,—as far as Lake Taupo, which is the centre of the island, and the largest of the New Zealand lakes. But though there are hot springs near Lake Taupo, and though the grandest jet of all, when it pleases to disport itself, is on Tongariro, a mountain to the south of Taupo, the traveller will see but little of that which he desires to see at the big lake[2].

Lakes Tarawera and Roto Mahana [Rotomahana] are in truth the spots of which he is in search, and they lie forty miles north of Lake Taupo. The second route is by the valley of the Waikato River, up which a coach runs from Auckland, as far as Cambridge, making the journey in two days. But Cambridge is ninety miles from Taupo, and about fifty from the district of the hot springs. The third route is by Tauranga, a seaport

---

1. Good roads now connect all the places mentioned here.
2. The hot springs are now harnessed for the supply of geo-thermal electric power.

on the Bay of Plenty, which is reached by steamer from Auckland in about twenty hours. From Tauranga, the lakes I have named lie about forty or fifty miles. In either direction, either from Taupo, Cambridge, or Tauranga, the journey must be made on horseback,—or on foot. Such was the condition of the places at the period of my visit,—but the road from Tauranga was being made through to Taupo, and when this is finished, the lakes and hot springs will be easily accessible.

I went by steamer from Auckland to Tauranga, thence I rode through the lakes down to Taupo and back to Cambridge, and returned to Auckland on wheels, having taken a fortnight for the excursion, during seven days of which I was in the saddle. We rode something over thirty miles a day, carrying such baggage as we required on our horses before us,—carrying during a portion of the journey, our provisions also. I was informed that any one desirous of seeing the lakes could hire horses and a competent guide at Tauranga. The trouble of doing this was taken off my hands, as I was accompanied by Captain Mair, of the Native Contingent, and by two orderlies, one a Maori and the other a European. There can, however, be but little doubt that in a year or two the trip will be made easy to all lovers of scenery, and that Roto Mahana and Tarawera will be reached from Auckland, if not so quickly, still as readily as Dartmoor or Windermere from London. . . .

From Tauranga we rode eighteen miles along the beach to Maketu, when I found myself in the midst of Maoris. These Maoris belong to the Arewa [Arawa] tribe, who were always friendly,—whereas at Tauranga the natives were hostile. Consequently the land around Tauranga has been confiscated, and divided among military settlers, whereas the Arewas still hold their ground,—not at all as far as one can see to the advantage of humanity at large.

At Maketu I walked up among the settlements, and shook hands with men and women, and smiled at them, and was smiled upon. At the inn they came and sat alongside of me,—so near that the contiguity sometimes almost amounted to an embrace. The children were noisy, jovial, and familiar. As far as one could judge, they all seemed to be very happy. There was a European schoolmaster there, devoted to the Maori children,—who spoke to me much of their present and future condition. He had great faith in their secular learning, but had fears as to their religious condition. He was most anxious that I should see them in school before I departed on the next morning, and I promised that I would do so. Though I was much hurried, I could not refuse such a request to a man so urgent in so good a cause. But in the morning, when I was preparing to be as good as my word, I was told that the schoolmaster had got very drunk after I had gone to bed, had smashed the landlord's windows, and had been carried away to his house by two policemen,—greatly, I hope, to the sorrow of those Maori scholars. After this little affair, it was not thought expedient that I should trouble him at an early hour on the following morning. I cannot but remark here that I saw very much more of drunkenness in New Zealand than in the Australian colonies; and I will remark, also, for the benefit of those who may ever visit these lakes, that there is a very nice little inn at Maketu.

On the following day we rode thirty-five miles, to Ohinemutu[1] through a very barren but by no means unpicturesque country. The land rises and falls in rapid little hills, and is tossed about in a wonderful fashion,—but there is no serious ascent or descent. The first lake seen is Roto Iti [Rotoiti], at the end of which we had to swim our horses across a river, passing over it ourselves in a canoe,—as we had done also at Maketu. And here at the end of the lake, we found a very fine Maori house, or whare,—I believe the word is properly so spelt, but it consists

---

1. Trollope, an ardent huntsman, was at home in the saddle.

of two syllables. And by the whare was a huge war-canoe, capable of carrying some sixty men at the paddles. These, as far as I could learn, were the property of the tribe, rather than of any individual. The whare was a long, low room, with high-pitched roof, with an earthen floor, and ornamented with grotesque and indecent carvings. I may, however, as well say that I doubt whether I should have discovered the indecency had it not been pointed out to me. I don't think anyone lived in the whare,—the chief of the tribe, as is usual, preferring his own little hut. No doubt had I wished to stay there, I might have slept on one of the mats with which a portion of the floor is covered.

Roto Iti, as I saw it, was very pretty, but I did not stop to visit the farther end of it, where, as I was told, the chief beauty of it lay. It may be as well to state that Roto is the Maori word for lake. We went on to Ohinemutu, passing a place called Ngae, on the lake Roto Rua [Rotorua],—whence according to the Maori legend, a Maori damsel, hearing the flute of her lover in the island Mokoia, swam off to him. As the distance is hardly more than a mile, and as the Maoris are all swimmers, the feat did not seem to me to be very wonderful,—till I heard that the flute was made out of the tibia of a man's leg[1]. At present there is a telegraph station at Ngae, and I found an unfortunate telegraphist living in solitude, inhabiting a small office on the lake side. Of course one took the opportunity of telegraphing to all one's friends, —but as visitors to Roto Rua are as yet but very scarce, I can hardly think that the station can pay its expenses.

On the farther side of Roto Iti I had seen great jets of steam at a distance. At Ohinemutu on Roto Rua, I came to the

---

1. It was not the feat, but the romantic circumstances, that make this one of the most celebrated of Maori legends. The full story is told in A. W. Reed's *Treasury of Maori Folklore*.

first hot springs which I saw closely, and I must own that at first they were not especially pleasing. Before reaching the spot we had to take our horses through the edge of the lake up to their bellies, at a place where the water was so impregnated with sulphur as to be almost unbearable on account of the stench. I had known the smell of sulphur before,—but here it seemed as though the sulphur were putrid.

Ohinemutu itself is a poor little Maori village, which seems to have collected itself round the hot springs, close on the borders of the lake, with a view to the boiling of potatoes without the trouble of collecting fuel. Here was a little inn, —or accommodation house as it is colonially called,—kept by a European with a half-caste wife, at which the traffic must be very small indeed. He appeared to be the only white inhabitant of the place, and I cannot say that I thought him to be happily placed in regard to his neighbours or neighbourhood. At Ohinemutu there is nothing pretty. The lake itself has no special loveliness to recommend it. But close upon its edge, there are numerous springs of boiling water,—so close that some of them communicate with the lake, making the water warm for some distance from the shore. There were half-a-dozen pools within a couple of hundred yards of the inn, in which you could boil potatoes or bathe at your will, choosing the heat which you thought desirable. Close beside the gate was one pool which is always boiling. My companion told me that a Maori man had come to him at that spot, desiring to be enlisted in the Maori Contingent. He was bound to refuse the recruit as being too old, whereupon the disappointed man threw himself into the pool and was boiled to death.

Along the path thence to the bathing-pool mostly frequented by the Maoris, there were various small jets here and there, some throwing up a little water, and others a little steam,— very suggestive of accidents in the dark. Such accidents are not

at all uncommon, the thin crust of earth not unfrequently giving
way and letting through the foot of an incautious wanderer into
a small boiling caldron below. Farther on there is the small
square pool, round and in which Maoris are always clustering;
—on which no European would, I should imagine, ever desire
to encroach, for the Maoris are many, and the waters are not
much. Above and around this, flat stones have been fixed on
the earth over steam-jets.—And here the Maoris squat and
talk, and keep themselves warm. They seem to become so fond
of the warmth as hardly to like to stir out of it. A little to
the left, there is a small landlocked cove of the lake in which
canoes were lying, and into which a hot spring finds its way,
—so that the water of the whole cove may perhaps average
ninety degrees of heat. Here on the following morning I bathed,
and found myself able to swim without being boiled. But on
the previous evening, about nine, when it was quite dark, I
had bathed in another pool, behind the inn. Here I had gone
in very light attire to make my first experience of these waters,
my friend the Captain accompanying me, and here we found
three Maori damsels in the pool before us. But this was nothing,
—nothing, at least, in the way of objection. The night was
dark; and if they thoroughly understood the old French proverb,
which has become royally English,[1] why should we be more
obstinate or less intelligent? I crept down into the pool, and as
I crouched beneath the water, they encouraged me by patting
me on the back. The place was black, and shallow, but large
enough for us all. I sat there very comfortably for half-an-hour
while they conversed with the Captain,—who was a Maori
scholar. Then I plunged into a cold river which runs into the
lake a few yards from the hot spring, and then returned to
the hot water amidst the renewed welcomings of the Maori
damsels. And so I passed my first evening among the geysers,
very pleasantly.

---

1. *Honi soit qui mal y pense.*

"Well, Mair, this is very delightful, don't you know, but I think I did wisely in leaving Mrs Trollope in Auckland."
(See a footnote by Captain Gilbert Mair, page 149.)

At Ohinemutu I saw nothing of uplifted columns of boiling water;—nor throughout the district did I see anything of the kind at all equal to the descriptions which I had read and heard. Indeed, I came across nothing which I could call a column of water thrown up and dispersed in the air. At some spots there were sudden eruptions, which would rise with a splutter rather than a column, perhaps six or eight feet high, —throwing boiling spray around, and creating an infinite quantity of steam; but these were not continuous, lasting perhaps a minute, and remaining quiescent for four or five, during which the rumbling and boiling of the waters beneath would be heard. In other places, jets of steam would be thrown up to a considerable height,—probably over twenty feet. As to the jets of water, I was told that I was unfortunate, and that the geysers were very tranquil during my visit. I have, however, observed all the world over, that the world's wonders, when I have reached them, have been less than ordinarily wonderful.

But I had not yet come to Roto Mahana, and was therefore not disappointed with Ohinemutu. Any deficiency in the geysers had been made up by the courtesy of the girls,—and it had been something to bathe in a lake, in water almost boiling me.

. . . On the next morning we rode up to a place called Wakare-warewa[1], about three miles from the lake, at which the sulphur, and the steam, and the noisy roaring boiling processes, were going on with great ferocity at various holes. Perhaps in some respects the thing is better realized as I saw it, than when columns of water are thrown up. I could stand and look down into the holes, and become thoroughly aware that a very slight spring, a step forward, would not only destroy me, but destroy me with terrible agony. All around me were small boiling pools,—for the most part delightfully blue,—each of which had its own boiling spring at the bottom. And among the pools

---

1. Whakarewarewa.

were great holes in the rocks, crusted with sulphur, out of which the geysers ought to have been lifting their heads, but down which indeed I could look, and see and hear the ferocious boiling waters. At Wakarewarewa there were no Maoris, and no inhabitants of any kind.

From thence we rode on past a beautiful little sheet of water called the Blue Lake to Kaiteriria, on another lake,— Roto Kahiki. Kaiteriria is the spot at which a certain number of the native contingent force,—the Maori soldiers in the pay of the government,—are kept, I cannot say in barracks, but in what I may perhaps call a Europeanised pah. The men live in huts of their own, but the huts are surrounded by a palisade, at the two gates of which Maori sentinels are stationed. The men are under the command of a European officer, who had two other Europeans with him in the depot. There seemed to be no danger of any disturbance among the men. As long as they are paid, and fed well, and not over-worked, these Arewa [Arawa] Maoris are too well alive to the advantages of their military service to risk them by mutiny or disobedience. The value attached to the service may be understood by the act of the man who boiled himself to death because he could not be admitted.

The entrance to Roto Mahana is by a beautiful little stream, which empties that lake into Tarawera, and Tarawera is about four miles from Kaiteriria. At the head of Tarawera,—which in point of scenery, is by far the finest of all these lakes, as Roto Mahana is the most interesting,—much had been done to form a civilised settlement of Maoris. There was a church, a clergy-man's house, a corn-mill, and a considerable extent of cleared land lying amid the beautifully broken ground. The church

was empty, and deserted[1]. The clergyman's house was falling
into decay, and was occupied by a Maori woman and a
Frenchman. The corn-mill was choked up, and in ruins. On
the land there was no sign of crop, or of preparation for crops.
Peach-trees had been planted in abundance,—and here and
there patches were bright with the pink peach-blossom. English
primroses were in full flower up at the parsonage. But everything was going back to the savageness of the wilderness. The
attempt had been made, and had been made among a friendly
tribe;—but it had failed, and the failure seemed to have been
acknowledged. There were Maoris in plenty,—a village full of
Maoris. When I asked how they lived, I was told that they
were Friendlies, and that therefore the Government fed them.
This Maori chief had a salary,—and that Maori chief. Then
there were men on the roads who received wages,—and the
sugar-and-flour policy was prevailing. It might be better to feed
them than to have to fight them.

I do not at all intend to find fault with the policy at present
pursued in regard to the Maoris,—neither with the existing
policy nor with any previous policy. I know the great difficulty
of the subject,—arising from our desire to do after some fashion
that shall be as little unjust as possible, a thing which according
to our light seems to be radically unjust from the beginning.
The attempt at justice has been so earnest that adverse criticism
is stopped. And anyone presuming to criticise should have had

---

1. Compulsory abandoned mission stations were among the
   tragedies of the Maori wars. This had been the mission station
   of the Rev. Mr Spencer who, with his family had several times
   been driven out by hostile Maoris, on the last occasion only a
   couple of years before Trollope saw it. "An old servant was
   living in a hut close by," said Captain Mair's sister Laura, when
   she visited the Terraces in 1873; "and she was delighted to see
   white folk in her old master's home. . . . Old Mary helped us
   with the cooking and housekeeping." (*Annals of a New Zealand
   Family.*)

much more opportunity of mastering the subject than has come my way. But I think that I could see that the race was not progressing towards civilisation, either with or without Christianity, as it was thought that they would progress. The people are dying out,—and thus and thus only, will the Maori difficulty be solved[1].

The deserted church and parsonage, with the Maori village, which no longer wanted a corn-mill because rations of flour and rations of biscuit were at their command, were most picturesquely placed among the hills from which we descended to Lake Tarawera. Here we found a canoe with three natives, our own party consisting of the Captain, two Europeans under his orders, and myself. The passage across the lake to the mouth of the little stream coming out of Roto Mahana, took us four hours. The shape of the lake is so fine, the mountains so well grouped, and the timber so good, that the spot will undoubtedly become famous with tourists on some future day, even if there were no hot lake near, and no geysers to attract holiday wanderers. Tarawera has this advantage among lakes,—that it is almost equally lovely on all sides. At the mouth of the river the Captain and I got out and walked to Roto Mahana, while the men worked the long canoe against the sharp stream, one or two of the natives getting into the water for the purpose. Before leaving the larger lake the water had gradually become warm, and in the river which came out from Roto Mahana it was almost tepid. For the hot springs round Roto Mahana are sufficiently numerous to warm the whole lake, which is small and irregularly formed, being perhaps a mile long and half a mile broad.

Here we found an incredible number of ducks,—as to which I was told that the Maoris do not approve of their being shot. In fact they are " tapu," or sacred by Maori law,—in order

---

1. This was the common belief at the time.

that they may be better preserved for a great slaughtering and preserving process which takes place once a year, in December. But the "tapu" in these days has become, even to Maoris themselves, a thing very much of pounds, shillings and pence, or of other material conditions. The "tapu" was taken off the ducks for the Duke of Edinburgh[1], when he visited Roto Mahana,—and might, I think, be lifted for a while to accommodate anyone who would pay high enough for a day or two's shooting.

It was nearly dark when we reached the lake,—there being just light enough for us to see the white terraces as we passed across the lower part of them. We were to eat our supper and sleep in a whare on the side of the lake, a little way from the terraces, in the midst of various steam-jets and water-jets. As I followed my leader through the bush I was cautioned not to step aside here, or to make a blunder there. In one place the Governor's aide-de-camp's dog had been boiled alive in a mud-jet, and in another a native girl had dropped a baby, and had herself plunged in after the poor infant,—hopelessly, tragically gone for ever amidst horrible torments.[2] I heard more, however, of the Governor's aide-de-camp's dog than I did of the girl and the baby. These mud-jets, or solfataras, are to be seen throughout the whole district, and are very far from being lovely. By some infernal chemistry, probably not very

---

1. Alfred Ernest Albert, second son of Queen Victoria (1844-1900). In 1869, when twenty-five years of age, he visited New Zealand. He was accompanied to the thermal regions by the Mair brothers, whose sister Laura tells us in *Annals of a New Zealand Family*, "My brothers found him a jolly companion, a good traveller, fair horseman in spite of his being a sailor, and always ready for a lark."

2. . . . yet,—if the dying words of some of them may be believed —not always agonizing, so completely does the shock of contact with the boiling water kill the nervous system." (William Pember Reeves, in *The Long White Cloud*).

low beneath the surface, earth and water are mixed, and are sent up in a boiling condition. When the aperture is small the mud simply boils and bubbles. When the mouth is large it is thrown up, and lies around in a great bubbling ring of dirt, soft and hot, and most damnable to any one who should place a foot upon it. Solfataras is a very pretty name, but the thing itself is very ugly both to the eye and to the imagination.

Our whare was close upon the lakeside, close also to various boiling springs. Here we cooked our bacon and potatoes, and then, when it was dark, crouched into a warm pool and sat there and enjoyed ourselves. When the water became too warm, I crept out into the lake, which was close at hand, with a barrier of stones dividing them, and which was warm also, though less warm than any of the pools. And then I got back again into the pool, conscious of the close vicinity of a naked Maori, who was supposed to see that I fell into no difficulties. But here the companions of the bath were of the less interesting sex, and I almost wished that they were away. The bathing was certainly good fun, but the night in the whare afterwards was less enjoyable. The ground was hard, the adjacent stream made the air hot and muggy,—and I had a feeling as of many insects.

The glory of Roto Mahana is in the terraces.[1] There are the white terraces on the side on which we had slept, and the pink

---

1. The pink and white terraces ranked amongst the loveliest of the world's scenic wonders. They were destroyed on June 10, 1886, when Mount Tarawera blew up, burying three native villages in the vicinity, and causing the death of about 150 people. From a scenic point of view this was New Zealand's greatest disaster. For countless years nature had been fashioning this masterpiece, which was destroyed in an instant. Comparatively few Europeans had looked upon these pink and white terraces, and very few indeed attempted written descriptions. It is likely that Anthony Trollope has given us our most detailed word-picture.

The Pink Terraces.
Sketched by Sid Scales from an early photograph.

terraces across the lake. I will endeavour in describing these to avoid any word that may seem to savour of science,—being altogether ignorant in such matters,—and will endeavour simply to say what I saw and felt. These terraces are formed of a soft, friable stone, which is deposited by the waters streaming down from the hot pools above. The white terraces are in form the finer of the two. They are about three hundred feet in width, and rise nearly two hundred in height, from the lake. As you ascend from the bottom you step along a raised fretwork of stone, as fine as chased silver. Among this the water is flowing, so that dry feet are out of the question, but the fret-work, if the feet be kept on it, assists the walker, as the water, though it runs over it, of course runs deeper through it. As you rise higher and higher, the water, which at the bottom is hardly more than tepid, becomes warmer and warmer. And then on one terrace after another there are large shell-like alabaster baths, holding water from three to four feet deep,—of different temperatures as the bather may desire them. Of course, the basins are not alabaster,—but are made of the deposit of the waters, which is, I believe, silica,—but they are as smooth as alabaster, only softer. And on the outside rims, where the water has run, dripping over, century after century, nature has carved for herself wonderful hanging ornaments and exquisite cornices, with that prolific hand which never stints itself in space because of expense, and devotes its endless labour to front and rear with equal persistency. On the top terrace is the boiling lake from whence the others are filled.

We had swum in Roto Mahana early in the morning, and did not bathe at the white terraces, having been specially recommended to reserve ourselves for those on the other side. So we crossed the lake to the pink terraces. In form, as I have said before, the white terraces are the finer. They are larger, and higher, and the spaces between the pools are more exquisitely worked,—and to my eye the colour was preferable. Both are in truth pink. Those which have the name of being so are brighter, and are salmon-coloured. They are formed after the same fashion, and the baths are constructed,—of course by

The White Terraces.
Sketched by Sid Scales from an early photograph.

nature,—in the same way. But those which we last visited were, I was told, more delicious to the bather. I can, indeed, imagine nothing more so. The bather undresses on a piece of dry rock a few yards distant, and is in his bath in half a minute without the chance of hurting his feet,—for it is one of the properties of the stone flooring which has here been formed that it does not hurt. In the bath, when you strike your chest against it, it is soft to the touch,—you press yourself against it and it is smooth,—you lie about upon it and, though it is firm, it gives to you. You plunge against the sides, driving the water over with your body, but you do not bruise yourself. You go from one bath to another, trying the warmth of each. The water trickles from the one above to the one below, coming from the vast boiling pool at the top, and the lower, therefore, are less hot than the higher. The baths are shell-like in shape,—like vast open shells, the walls of which are concave, and the lips of which ornamented in a thousand forms. Four or five may sport in one of them, each without feeling the presence of the other. I have never heard of other bathing like this in the world.

And from the pink terraces, as you lie in the water, you look down upon the lake which is close beneath you, and over upon the green broken hills which come down upon the lake. The scene here, from the pink terraces, is by far the lovlier, though the white terraces themselves are grander in their forms. It is a spot for intense sensual enjoyment, and there comes perhaps some addition to the feeling from the roughness you must encounter leaving it. The time probably will soon come in which there will be a sprightly hotel at Roto Mahana, with a table d'hote, and boats at so much an hour, and regular seasons for bathing. As I lay there, I framed the programme of such a hotel in my mind,—and I did so, fixing the appropriate spot as I squatted in the water, and calculating how much it would cost, and what return it would give. I was somewhat troubled by the future bathing arrangements. To enclose the various basins would spoil them altogether to the eye. To dabble about in vestments arranged after some French fashion would spoil the bathing to the touch. And yet it must be open to men and women alike. The place lies so broad to the world's eye that I fear no arrangement as to hours, no morning for the gentlemen and evening for the ladies, would suffice. Alas, for the old Maori simplicity and perfect reliance on the royal adage! The ladies, indeed, might have the pink, and the men the white terraces; but the intervening lake would discourage social intercourse;—and there would be interlopers and intruders who might break through the " tapu " of modern propriety.

After bathing we went to the top, and walked round the hot spring from which the water descends. It has formed a lake about a quarter of a mile in circumference, the waters of which are constantly boiling, and are perfectly blue. In the centre it is said to be many feet deep. The colour is lovely, but in order to see it we had to get behind the wind, so that the steam should not be blown into our faces. As we came down we found parts of the crusted floor perfectly yellow with pure sulphur, and parts of the fretted stone-work on the under curves of the rocks, where they were not exposed to the light, as perfectly green. Then there were huge masses brightly salmon-coloured, and here and there delicately-white fretwork, and the lips and sides of the baths were tinted with the delicate pink hue which we are apt to connect with soft luxury.

We returned across the small warm lake, and down the rapid river,—which has some Maori name meaning the "breaking of canoes," derived from the accidents occasioned by the rapid windings of the stream; and we were rowed again across the great Lake Tarawera to the deserted chapel and the broken corn-mill,—and thence we walked to Kaiteriria, where I slept amidst the Native Contingents.

Having done this I had really seen the hot springs of the province of Auckland, and I would advise no traveller who is simply desirous of seeing them to go farther south. One cannot travel through any part of that wild country without seeing much that is worth seeing, and south of Roto Mahana or of Kaiteriria there are many steam-jets and geysers. As I have said before, the greatest geyser of all, when it chooses to play, is on Tongariro, south of Lake Taupo. But jets of boiling water, and jets of steam, and jets of mud, though they are wonderful, are hardly in themselves beautiful,—and in the neighbourhood of Ohinemutu and of Roto Mahana there are enough to gratify even an ardent curiosity. But I had made my plans to see Lake Taupo, and to return by the valley of the Waikato, and this I did. From Kaiteriria to Taupo it was a long day's work,—the distance of which we increased from forty-five to fifty miles by losing our way. On the route we passed a hot river in which we bathed,—a river which became hot at a certain point by the operation of a boiling spring, and then cooled itself by degrees,—so that the bather might wade into hotter or into cooler water as he might wish. Fifteen miles beyond this we crossed, for the first time, the Waikato River, which in the lower part of its course had been the scene of so much fighting, and here we left the friendly Arewa [Arawa] tribe and got among the Wharetowa [Wharetoa], who, in the time of the war were our foes. When we crossed the river we found a village, and another close to the lake,—looking poor, miserable, and dirty. At ten o'clock at night we crossed back over the Waikato, and found ourselves at the town of Tapuaeharu, which consists of a large redoubt held by European armed constabulary, and of an inn. There were a few Maori whares round about, but they clustered chiefly on the side of the river we had just left.

I crossed the lake, which is about twenty-five miles long and twenty-two broad, in a boat rowed by six constables, and put up for the night at the Maori village of Takano [Tokaanu] at the other end. The country all round,—as it had been indeed since we left Maketu, with the exception of small patches at the head of Tarawera,—was not only uncultivated, but apparently barren and poor by its nature. The ordinary growth is a low stunted fern, which sometimes gives place to tufts of thick yellow grass. I was told that sheep had been tried upon it in places, but that they had fallen off and had perished. The attempt had been a failure. At Tokano there was a large village, and here I found in the valley of the river some potato patches. The land was better than it had been beyond the lake; but I saw nothing that savoured either of prosperity or of civilisation. Old tattooed natives came and grinned at me. Young women, tattooed, as are all the women, on the under-lip, sat close to me and chattered to me; and young men kindly shook me by the hand. I encountered nothing but Maori friendship; —but at the same time I encountered no Maori progress. As I had not time to go on to Tongariro I returned on the next day to the other end of the lake,—and during the following three days I rode to Cambridge, a new little town on the lower Waikato.

The distance is about ninety miles, and a more desolate country it would be hard to imagine. In the first eighty miles there is not a sign of cultivation. The land is fern-covered, and is very poor, and is not yet in the hands of Europeans. During the whole distance we descended the course of the Waikato, though at some places we were miles away from it. Our first night we spent at another depot of the native contingent force, in a collection of huts similar to that at Kaiteriria. Here again we bathed in a warm spring close to the river, and here again we crossed the Waikato in a canoe.

Some of the scenery on this route was certainly very fine. We passed through one winding gorge, with the rocks high above our heads, which seemed to be the very spot for another Thermopylae. And in certain places the river had made for itself a grand course, rushing down rapids, and cutting a deep channel for itself between narrow banks. But the desolation of the country was its chief characteristic. There were no men or women, and nothing on which men and women could live. There were no animals,—hardly even a bird to be seen, till as we came near to European haunts, we occasionally put up one of the pheasants with which the lower Waikato has been stocked. There is perhaps no country in the world more destitute of life than the wilder parts of the North Island of New Zealand. During one long day a wild cat was the only animal we saw, after leaving the neighbourhood of the place from which we started. On that night we slept at a Maori pah, which we did not reach till dark,—and before reaching it we had to pass through a dense wood in darkness so thick that I could not see my hand. I mention the fact in order that I may express my wonder at the manner in which my friend the Captain made way through it[1]. That night I had a small Maori hut all to myself,—one in which were deposited all the tokens of recent Maori habitation. There was a little door just big enough for ingress,—hardly big enough for egress,—and a heap of fern leaves, and a looking-glass, and a bottle which looked like perfumery,—and the feeling as of many insects. In the morning two old women cooked some potatoes for us,—and I rode away, intending never to spend another night among the Maoris.

They are certainly more highly gifted than other savage nations I have seen. They are as superior in intelligence and courage to the Australian Aboriginal as they are in outward appearance. They are more pliable and nearer akin in their manners to civilised mankind than are the American Indians. They are more manly, more courteous, as more sagacious than the African negro. One can understand the hope and the ambition of the first great old missionaries who had dealings with them. But contact with Europeans does not improve them.

---

1. Captain Mair was thoroughly familiar with this part of the country, the scene of his years'-long pursuit of Te Kooti.

At the touch of the higher race they are poisoned and melt away. There is scope for poetry in their past history. There is room for philanthropy as to their present condition. But in regard to their future,—there is hardly a place for hope. . . .

The military settlers have not generally succeeded as farmers in New Zealand,—but the general process has been successful. After a short period of occupation, the old soldiers were enabled to sell their lands, and have very generally done so. The purchasers have gone upon it with true colonising intentions, and now the upper part of the Lower Waikato, and the Valley of the Waipa which runs into it, the districts round the new towns of Cambridge, Alexandra [Pirongia], Hamilton and Newcastle [Ngaruawahia], are smiling with English grasses. I was there in 1872; the first occupation of it by Europeans had been in 1865; and the wilderness had become a garden. I do not know that I have ever seen the effects of a quicker agricultural transformation. This has been effected on the land of natives who had been hostile and had fought with us, and who had therefore lost their possessions, Among the Arewas, "the Friendlies," I did not see one cultivated patch of ground.

Coming down the Waikato during our last day's ride, the king's country had been on our left, just over the river. I had been told, and I believe truly, that a European might now travel through it safely if he wore no uniform or were not ostensibly armed. And among the Kingites, as they are now called, a certain amount of agriculture is now carried on. They want potatoes and corn, and cannot get them by other means. The question now is whether they shall be allowed to die out on their own territory,—which is claimed by us as British territory, but in which the British law, or the law of the colony, does not run, in which we cannot put up a telegraph wire or make a road,—or whether we shall make good our claims to political dominion? In the meantime the natives in these parts still hold the escaped criminal Te Kooti, in endeavouring to retake whom we have spent something like half a million of money, and may on any day make a raid on our advanced settlers on the Waikato and Waipa. All politicians in New Zealand find consolation at any rate in the reflection, that while the matter is being considered, the Maoris are melting. The flour-and-sugar policy[1], joined with the melting policy, will probably carry the day to the end.

A party of gentlemen from Auckland met me at Cambridge, which is, as it were, the frontier settlement of civilisation in that direction. From thence we were driven by Mr Quick, that gallant American coach proprietor and true descendant of the great Cobb, through Ohaupo to Alexandra [Pirongia], thence to Hamilton, Newcastle [Ngaruawahia], Rangiriri, fatally known to British arms during the war[2], and then on through Mercer and Drury, back to Auckland. During the earlier part of this journey, and down to the junction of the Waipa and Waikato at Newcastle, we were for the most part among fields green with English grasses. The fern which, throughout the district had occupied the land, is first burned off, the land is then ploughed, and grass seeds are sown. Then in two years' time it will carry five, six, and on some ground seven sheep to the acre. I saw very little wheat farming, and was told here,—as I was in all parts of the Northern Island,—that it did not pay to grow cereal crops. A man might produce what oats he could use,—and what wheat he wanted if he had a mill near him. But the high rate of wages,—averaging over 4s a day,—and the cost of transit combined, make the farmers afraid of wheat. Though the land is excellent for the purpose, and the climate

---

1. The flour-and-sugar policy is the nickname given to the practice by which the Government bribes into submission (A. T.'s note).
2. The scene of a desperate fight. 183 Maori prisoners were taken after severe losses on both sides. It was these prisoners who were sent to Kawau Island, and who escaped to the mainland, and eventually succeeded in getting back to their homes.

not unpropitious, I saw on the road flour, imported into Auckland, on its way up to those agricultural settlements. As in most of the Australian colonies, so in most of the New Zealand provinces, farmers who no doubt know what they are about, are afraid of growing wheat. They cannot get in their seed, and get their crops off without hired labour,—and for hired labour wheat at 5s a bushel will not enable them to pay. The labourer with his 4s a day will get more out of the crop than the farmer who employs him. Meat is at present the great produce of the Waikato valley,—for sheep and oxen will feed themselves if there be grass, and will then carry themselves kindly to the market. All English fruits grow there, and all vegetables. It is a country of great abundance,—and the day will come when the valley will be yellow with corn.

At Alexandra, which is the European outpost in the direction of the Ngatimaniapoto tribe and the Kingites,—and which is so near the "King" country that a moderate walk of three or four miles will place you in his Majesty's dominions,—we found a large fort or redoubt in the course of construction. It was being made, we were told, as a place of refuge for the inhabitants, should the king's people ever attempt to make a raid upon the town. "It would be the saving of the lives of all the women and children," said one of my companions. I could not help thinking that I would not like to live in a place where such refuge[1] might be necessary,—and that it was a pity that it should still be necessary in any part of her Majesty's dominions. The inhabitants, however, seemed to fear nothing, and were of opinion that the Kingites would not come down upon them. I found the feeling to be general throughout the islands that if the property now left to the natives were respected,—not only in regard to those rights of property which belong to individual owners in all civilised lands, but also as to political rights,—if

1. It was never required as such.

the Europeans should not insist on extending their dominion, as they would do, for instance, if they were to continue their attempts to retake Te Kooti,—then there would be peace; but that the Kingites would surely fight, should we practically assume dominion over the small portion of the Northern Island still left to them. Some time since the Governor thought it would be expedient that he should meet the king, on friendly terms. But the king thought otherwise,—"What have I to do with the Governor, or the Governor with me?" So there was no meeting.

Rangariri [Rangiriri], where the fighting took place in 1863,— where the natives held two redoubts when General Cameron attacked them, and escaped from the one in the night, surrendering the other on the following morning, after a terrible slaughter inflicted on our men,—is on the Waikato, below Newcastle [now Ngaruawahia]. Here again I saw the crowded graves of British soldiers, and the wooden memorials, bearing the name of each, already mouldering into dust. The redoubts are now but heaps of earth, one of which is already hardly discernible by the remnants of the rifle-pits which remain.

From this, down to Mercer, and nearly as far as Drury,— so-called from my old friend and school-fellow, Captain Drury,

---

1. Trollope was mistaken in crediting Drury with selecting the site for Auckland city.

Captain Byron Drury was commander of H.M.S. *Pandora,* employed in coastal surveys in northern New Zealand in the 1850's. Canon J. W. Stack, then a youth employed on Archdeacon Maunsel's mission station on the lower Waikato, has an interesting reference to Trollope's old schoolfellow, who, with his wife, paid a visit to the mission station. "The naval party spent a week with us while surveying the mouth of the river. One day they met a large canoe, paddled by the same number of men as the boat contained. The Maoris challenged the boat's crew to race them to the heads, distant about seven miles.

(See next page.)

Lord Byron's godson, who surveyed the coasts in these parts, and selected the site of the capital,[1]—the land is again poor. There is now a railway in course of construction from Auckland up to Mercer,[2] and from thence there is water-carriage by the two rivers to Cambridge and Alexandra. That the colony can afford to make these railways, I will not take upon myself to say. The making of them is a part of that grand go-ahead policy of which Mr Vogel is the eminent professor. That the Waikato district will be benefited by the railway when it is made there can be no doubt whatever.

I returned to Auckland under Mr Quick's able guidance, and then my wanderings in these colonies were over. Three days afterwards I shipped myself on board the famous American steamer "Nebrasca," Captain Harding, and was carried safely by him as far as Honolulu, among the Sandwich Islands, on my way home.

The challenge was accepted, and the canoe soon shot ahead. But the steady stroke of the men-of-war's men readily caught it up again. Then for about five miles the Maoris succeeded in spurting past the boat every time it came up to them. Then the sailors put forth all their strength, got the lead, and reached the landing place a mile ahead of the canoe. We were very glad it was so, for it checked the growing spirit of bumptiousness which was beginning to appear amongst the younger Maoris, who regarded themselves as physically superior to the English. Now they had to admit that they were beaten in a fair trial of strength." (*More Maoriland Adventures*. Ed. A.H.R.).

A few years later, during the Waikato war, the *Pandora* was stationed at Onehunga, and Commander Drury was responsible for delivery of supplies to the military base which bears his name.

2. Some years later permission was given for the railway to traverse the King Country. The Auckland-Wellington main trunk railway was completed in 1907.

Auckland Looks at Anthony

THE *Daily Southern Cross* of the 14th September, 1872 announced: "Mr Anthony Trollope arrived in Auckland yesterday morning, having reached Onehunga from Wellington by the 'Phoebe'. Mr Trollope was visited by his Worship the Mayor, who, after congratulating him upon his safe arrival, and offering him a cordial welcome to the city, presented a letter from Mr J. Pond, Honorary Secretary of the Auckland Mechanics' Institute, as follows:

Auckland, September 13, 1872.

"Sir,—The committee of the Auckland Mechanics' Institute desire to offer you a hearty welcome to this city, and, as a memento of your visit, respectfully ask permission to enrol your name among the honorary members of the Institute. The Mechanics' Institute, founded for the diffusion of knowledge among the inhabitants of Auckland in the early days of the colony, has had to struggle through times of great difficulty; but the committee look forward to its forming the foundation of a public library worthy of the city, with which they will be proud to see your name has been connected. I have, &c., J. POND."

"His Worship expressed a hope that Mr Trollope would favour the people of Auckland with a lecture before leaving the province. It would be looked forward to as a source of great pleasure by the citizens. Mr Trollope replied by saying that it was his intention to visit the interior of the province, when upon his return he would be able to say whether it would be in his power to comply with the wish expressed by Mr Philips. Mr Trollope will leave for Tauranga by the steamer 'Southern Cross' on Monday next and will proceed from thence to the Lake district."

Philip Aaron Philips (1831-1913) was one of the leaders of the Jewish community in Auckland. In 1867 he became Auckland's first mayor, and was also president of the Mechanics' Institute. He served again as mayor 1871-1874, when he retired

139

and was appointed town clerk, a position which he occupied for a quarter of a century.

"Mr Anthony Trollope arrived yesterday in the *Phoebe* from Wellington," stated the *New Zealand Herald* on Saturday, September 14. . . . "He is the guest of Dr Campbell. Several of the principal citizens were invited last evening to meet him. His stay in Auckland will be very brief. . . . The Mayor and Town Clerk waited on him yesterday with the view of inducing him to give a public lecture during his stay in Auckland. Mr Trollope said he was not able to give an immediate reply, but he would bear the representations to him in mind. . . ."

"Mr Anthony Trollope," said the same newspaper on Tuesday the 17th, "visited the Provincial Secretary, Mr H. H. Lusk, yesterday afternoon, for the purpose of obtaining statistical information regarding the present conditions of native affairs. It is to be hoped Mr Lusk put a good face on the matter, in view of the future book in which we are all to be shown up. It is not in every part of the world that the book-maker can see a specimen of a Provincial Secretary."

Anthony Trollope's Novels

To the Editor of the New Zealand Herald

(Thursday, September 19)

"Sir,—Will you permit me, through the medium of your columns, to correct a statement made in the *Southern Cross* of this day, in reference to the above, as I have still a large number of this popular author's works on hand, including—The Belton Estate, The Bertrams, Can You Forgive Her, Castle Richmond, Dr Thorne, He Knew He was Right, The Kellys and the O'Kellys, Lotto Schmidt, The McDermotts of Ballycloran, Mary Gresley, Miss Mackenzie, Orley Farm, Phineas Finn, Rachel Ray, Tales of All Countries—and will be glad to dispose of them, as I have more ordered to arrive. I am, etc., G. H. CHAPMAN, Bookseller. 'Auckland, September 18, 1872'."

"The following letter has been received by Mr J. A. Pond," stated the *Daily Southern Cross* of Tuesday the 17th:

Auckland, September 15, 1872.

"My dear Sir,—Mr Philips has handed me your note of the 13th instant. I wish it were in my power to comply with your flattering request, but my time in Auckland will not permit of my doing so. I start tomorrow (Monday) for the hot wells, and hardly know when I may be back—barely, I fear, in time to catch the boat for San Francisco, which is said to start on the 3rd proximo. I could not give a lecture without passing a day, and devoting some unreasonable time to the preparation of it. As it is, my attention is almost more than fully occupied with my endeavours to learn something of the British settlements which I am visiting. I trust that you will not think that I am uncourteous.—Yours, &c., ANTHONY TROLLOPE."

During Mr Trollope's excursion in the interior, Mrs Trollope remained in Auckland, and when he was on his way back to the city, the *Daily Southern Cross,* had this to say, on Thursday, September 26:

"We understand that the members of the Provincial Government are endeavouring to make the visit of Mr Anthony Trollope to this province both a profitable and a pleasurable one. For some time past, as is well known, Mr Trollope has been enjoying himself amid the unrivalled scenery of the Lake district, in this province. He has decided to come overland from Lake Taupo to Cambridge, and yesterday afternoon we understand the Deputy-Superintendent and the Provincial Secretary in company with Dr Campbell left town to meet Mr Trollope at Cambridge, on his arrival there. It will be their endeavour to show Mr Trollope the various scenes in the Waikato district of historic interest, and to relate to him the legends, traditions, and tales of blood and carnage associated with each. If the various events of the late war are carefully related to Mr Trollope, and the positions occupied by the armies of civilisation and barbarism in the several engagements pointed out, a vast fund of material will be placed at his disposal which may be before long woven into a story that will tend to make New Zealand better known to the British public than she has yet been. The bibliography of New Zealand is already an extensive one, but when our unrivalled scenery—now made accessible to the tourist through peace having been restored—becomes better known to British authors, the list of published books upon this colony will rapidly increase. The results flowing from a greater familiarity with New Zealand cannot be otherwise than favourable to the colony, and the most effectual way to secure this is to place full and accurate information at the disposal of those authors of eminence who may visit our shores. By doing so the tide of immigration and of sight-seeing will soon flow towards us, and by gaining a more exact knowledge of New Zealand those stupid blunders, geographical and others, which are too often made at present by British writers, both for the newspapers and periodical press, will be avoided. The gentlemen who left town yesterday expect to meet Mr Trollope about Friday, and at least a week will be spent examining the various places of interest in the Waikato district, and in the journey to town."

"Dr Campbell" was, of course John (later Sir John) Logan Campbell (1817-1912) "the Father of Auckland," pioneer benefactor who, in addition to many other gifts, presented the city with the 300 acres known as Cornwall Park.

It is much to be regretted that the hopes expressed by the writer in the *Southern Cross,* and felt by many others, were never realised. The Trollopes' main reason for visiting Australia was to visit their son Frederic, who had several years previously, emigrated to New South Wales, where he settled as a sheep farmer, and reared what has been described as a "patriarchal family." Trollope wrote his short story, *Harry Heathcote of Gangoil* in 1874, and the novel *John Caldigate,* in 1879, both with an Australian background. With the material he had gathered, he might have given us a classic novel with a New

Zealand setting. His novels have merely passing references to New Zealand.

It would appear that Mr Trollope was interviewed on his return to Auckland. The *Daily Southern Cross* of October 2 headed its report:

Mr Anthony Trollope returns from the Interior

"It will be remembered that a fortnight ago last Monday Mr Anthony Trollope was a passenger per p.s. 'Southern Cross' for Tauranga, en-route to the Lakes, and the Taupo and Waikato districts. The Governor placed the services of Major Gilbert Mair[1] at Mr Trollope's disposal on his arrival at Tauranga, and he had therefore the advantage of an intelligent gentleman, thoroughly acquainted with that part of the province, as his guide. Mr Trollope arrived at Tauranga on Tuesday, and started inland on Wednesday. It is needless to say that Mr Trollope was pleased with the natural wonders he saw in the Lake region. The district is without a parallel in the world, and the more one meditates on the scene around him there the more enraptured he becomes with the unrivalled beauties of the place. From the Lake region he proceeded on to Lake Taupo. The country around Taupo was examined and he

---

1. Two sons of the pioneer Gilbert Mair (1797-1857) distinguished themselves in the Maori wars: Major William Gilbert Mair (1832-1912), and his younger brother Captain (not Major) Gilbert Mair (1843-1923). It was Captain Mair who guided Trollope through the Hot Lakes district. During the Maori war he was conspicuous both for courage and humanity. During an engagement he carried out a wounded chief under fire, and on another occasion risked his life to succour a wounded follower of the notorious Te Kooti. It was for conspicuous gallantry while leading his Arawa "friendlies" against Te Kooti in 1870 (so near to the period of Trollope's visit) that Captain Mair was awarded the New Zealand Cross, the equivalent of the Victoria Cross, and ranking next to that in precedence.

proceeded one-and-a-half days' journey inland, towards Tonga-riro, but the party did not ascend the mountain. From Taupo they made their way overland to Cambridge, which place they reached last Friday evening. There Mr Trollope was joined by Dr J. L. Campbell; the Deputy-Superintendent, Mr Joseph May[1]; and the Provincial Secretary, Mr H. H. Lusk[2]. The weather was excellent all the time that Mr Trollope was in the interior, and a change only occurred after his arrival in the Waikato district. The party who met him at Cambridge accompanied him around a portion of that district to show what the labour of a small body of Anglo-Saxons had accomplished in a few years of comparative peace. They drove round by Alexandra, and thence to Hamilton, and reached Auckland on Monday afternoon, after having been just a fortnight absent. We understand that Mr Trollope is much pleased with the natural beauties which he has witnessed, and especially by the progress made by the settlers in the Waikato. It seemed even to those who were with him that it was scarcely possible that such great progress could have been made in so short a time since the district was only the abode of savages. The progress made by New Zealand is most marked, and we are warranted in saying that Mr Trollope is already convinced that New Zealand has little in common with the colonies on the mainland of Australia. In time we shall doubtless have the pleasure of reading his matured opinion on the comparative futures of which the cluster of colonies usually known by the name of the Australasian colonies will severally attain. Love for our adopted country makes us hope, and its past history convinces us that Mr Trollope will not assign to New Zealand

1. Joseph May (1816-1890) was elected Deputy-Superintendent of the Auckland Province in 1870, and later represented the Franklin electorate in Parliament.
2. Hugh Hart Lusk (1837-1926) founded a legal practice in Auckland, was elected to the provincial Council in 1870, and succeeded Joseph May in Parliament in 1876.

the lowest position in that galaxy of nations which is springing
up around us. Yesterday we understand that Mr Trollope,
accompanied by Dr Campbell, visited the Titirangi district,
for the purpose of seeing some large kauri trees, and the general
appearance of a kauri forest. Several trees from 8ft to 9ft
diameter were seen even in this district, which has been under-
going a process of depletion for the last 30 years; this must
be taken as an indication of what a forest in New Zealand is.
This evening Mr Trollope will be entertained at dinner by the
members of the Northern Club, and he will leave our shores
by the 'Nebrasca'."

Banquet to Mr Anthony Trollope
Mr Trollope's Experience of the Colonies

"In our issue of yesterday morning," stated the *Southern Cross*
of October 3, "we intimated that Mr Anthony Trollope was
to be entertained by the members of the Northern Club at
dinner last night. This took place in superb style. About 44
gentlemen sat down to dinner, the table being most tastefully
decorated with vari-coloured flowers, &c. The chair was
occupied by Sir George Alfred Arney[1], Chief Justice, and the
vice-chair by Captain Daveney. A considerable number of
toasts were proposed, and responded to. The chairman, in
proposing the toast of the evening, the health of their guest,

---

1. Sir G. A. Arney (1810-1883) was born at Salisbury, England,
   in 1857 was appointed Chief Justice of New Zealand, and
   when he arrived at Auckland in 1858 was the only judge in the
   colony, Scholefield (Dictionary of New Zealand Biography)
   describes him as "an able lawyer, absolutely impartial, a man
   of great refinement, and a Christian gentleman; modern in his
   outlook, gentle almost to timidity, a lover of the classics and
   art." The opinion, expressed by Sir George, that New Zealanders
   were better patrons of literature than were people in the older
   countries, and Trollope's confirmation, have been borne out in
   succeeding years.

Mr Anthony Trollope, made allusion to the influence of literature, and its especial bearing upon colonial communities. He considered that, compared with old-established countries such as England, new countries like New Zealand, if estimated on a population basis were better patrons of literature than older and more populous lands. Mr Trollope, in responding to the toast that had been drunk, expressed himself pleased with the kindness which had been shown to him in Auckland and the other places in New Zealand which he had visited. He expressed his gratitude for the kind hospitality of which he had that night partaken. It had been the same everywhere in the colonies, an amount of kindness and marked respect had been paid to him which he did not expect to receive, and which he could never have anticipated on leaving England. When in England he moved in those circles of society where it was customary to show marked respect to favourite authors. . . . But on leaving England for the Australasian colonies he expected to come among men earnest in their struggle to reclaim a wilderness—earnest in carving out of the primeval forests homes for themselves and their families, with but little time and less inclination to pay attention to literature. But what were the facts he found on a personal examination. All through the wide extent of Australia, and in every house in New Zealand he had been in, he not only found some of his own works, but many of the works of Thackeray, Dickens and other authors of eminence in all the walks of literature, and he had become convinced that on a population basis the colonies had more warm patrons of literature than even the old country with all its riches.

"He referred to the indebtedness of New Zealand, and said since he had come here he had become convinced that New Zealand owed a great deal of money, and that her colonists knew well how to borrow. But they had no reason to be discouraged, for France, America, Germany and England, each and all owed a great deal of money. Estimated, however, upon the populations of the several countries, he thought that New Zealand was by far the largest debtor. But while he admitted that New Zealanders knew how to borrow money, he had seen enough to convince him that they knew also how to spend it satisfactorily. He could not but look back upon the roads he had seen made and in progress, in different parts of the colony, the railways that had been constructed, and those planned, and the relation those roads and railways held to the settled districts of the colony, without being assured that, if those colonising agencies were faithfully carried out, a great future awaited New Zealand, and that they would repay two-fold all her borrowed money[1]. It was the faithful expenditure of the borrowed money hitherto that had raised the credit of the colony so high in the old country; and while the same judicious mode of expenditure was observed there would be no want of money on applying for it in England. He looked upon this country as a remarkably fast country. It had done, in its short history, what no other country had done. It had acquired its lands by fair means, by fair purchase from the natives, and, as they had begun justly, he hoped they would continue to act justly in the future. It was the fairness observed by the New Zealand colonists in their dealings with the natives that had raised the colony and its inhabitants so high in the esteem of the old country, and when the facts were made a little better known the colony would suffer nothing by it. . . .

"He referred very briefly to the scenery he had seen, to the marks of progress he had witnessed in various districts, and expressed a hope that whatever political changes might occur in New Zealand, no separation of the two islands would ever take place. He wished to see the country remain a united whole. The climate of New Zealand he much admired, and the general

---

1. New Zealand was in the process of spending Sir Julius Vogel's borrowed millions.

hospitality of the people was characteristic. . . . The large un-
developed resources were briefly referred to, and he concluded
with the remark that what he had seen in New Zealand, and
his thoughts upon the progress she had made in her brief career,
yet remained to be told. Mr Trollope was repeatedly and
warmly cheered while he was speaking upon his colonial
experiences."

The *New Zealand Herald* had little to say about Mr Trollope
after his return from the interior. On the 2nd October his New
Zealand pilgrimage was described as "a flying visit indeed."

A brief reference to the dinner at the Northern Club states:
"The affair was of a private nature, no invitation having been
issued to the press." Was this omission an oversight, or did the
Southern Cross gatecrash the banquet?

In a final glimpse of the tireless traveller the *New Zealand
Herald* tells us that on the very morning that he embarked,
Trollope visited the Supreme Court in company with Dr
Campbell.

Mr and Mrs Trollope left Auckland for England, via
Honolulu and San Francisco, on Thursday, October 3. In those
days the mail steamer apparently had to lie out in the harbour,
for a shipping notice in the *Daily Southern Cross* advised the
Nebrasca passengers that the p.s. *Enterprise,* carrying passengers
and baggage, would leave the wharf at 11 a.m.

During their homeward voyage Trollope worked steadily at
his book, for which he received £1,300. Journey's end was
reached in December 1872, and the bulky volume, *Australia
and New Zealand,* appeared a few months later. As was the
case with some of his other books, it met with a somewhat mixed
reception. The *Athenaeum* and *Saturday Review* were critical
of its length, diffuseness and want of method, but *The Times*
described it as "the most agreeable, just and acute work ever
written on the subject."

A Footnote by Captain Gilbert Mair

Captain Gilbert Mair was only twenty-nine years of age when he guided Trollope though the then little-known thermal regions. He was then nearly thirty years Trollope's junior, and many years later, in his *Reminiscences* issued half a century later by the Brett Publishing Company, he gives us an entertaining account of his experiences with the hunting novelist.

". . . I met him by arrangement at Tauranga. He was a typical and jovial John Bull in appearance, with his breeches and gaiters, very stout and hearty, downright in manners, and brusque. A, fine type of Englishman, an excellent rider and judge of horseflesh, and he never tired of relating stories of the hunting field. And he hated snobs and society snobbishness with a deadly hatred. . . . In his little book *Our Antipodes* . . . [Here follows a short passage corresponding with Trollope's own story of bathing with Maori damsels at Ohinemutu]. But Mr Trollope discreetly omitted one little episode from his chronicles. After we had been in the water some time the old chap said, 'I wish I had something to lean against,' and so I whispered to a fine young woman of splendid proportions, popularly known as 'the Duchess,' who immediately set her capacious back against him, whereat he exclaimed, 'Well, Mair, this is very delightful, don't you know, but I think I did wisely in leaving Mrs Trollope in Auckland[1].

---

1. At this point Mair quotes from what he describes as Trollope's " little book," *Our Antipodes*. A mystery surrounds this title. Hocken knows nothing of it, nor does Sadlier in his bibliography, nor the Alexander Turnbull Library, nor the Dunedin Public Library. Mair's quotation is, "I knew then why the Maori

(See next page.)

"We returned to Auckland by way of Cambridge . . . a rough and ready township, with a large constabularly station. . . . The waitress came to ask me what we would like for breakfast. 'Bacon and eggs for two,' I replied. My friend had already whispered that thirteen of us had sat down to tea, and curiously enough the remaining eleven all ordered the same meal. Our breakfast table was about forty feet long, and the guests were scattered haphazard from end to end. There was only one mustard pot, and whether it was colonial snobbery or politeness I cannot say, but the whole eleven boarders vied with each other as to who would be first in tendering the mustard. Mr Trollope gruffly thanked the first to offer it, gave a deep grunt at the second, and a suppressed roar at the third. At last one boarder rose up from the faraway end, and bowing courteously enquired 'May I offer you the mustard, Sir?' The literary giant sprang to his feet and bellowed, 'Damn your eyes, Sir—Look at me! Do I look physically incapable of getting what mustard I require?' The too-polite boarder fell back in his chair, and there was a terrific silence, only to be broken when Mr Trollope grunted to me, 'Mair, I was a damn fool to sit down with thirteen at a table.' I could not help laughing outright, and he followed; then the whole baker's dozen set the roof shaking with laughter. Much hearty hand-shaking followed, and he said farewell to us all and went his way. Before he departed he made me promise that if ever I visited England he would make me follow the hounds with his 500-guinea hunter. That, alas, was one of the many beautiful dreams that have never come true."

---

boiled himself to death because he was not admitted to the force." This particular sentence does not appear in either the English or Australian edition of Trollope's book. Could Mair have quoted from one of Trollope's letters written to the English press under that heading, and in the lapse of time assumed it to have appeared in a "little book?" Could Trollope have written a " little book" for private circulation? After nearly a century it appears to remain a minor bibliographical mystery.

In 1875 when the Trollopes visited Australia for the second time, to see their grandchildren, the vessel put in for a few hours only at Auckland.

Journeys to the Continent and to South Africa were undertaken during the seventies, and several novels were published. Altogether Trollope received about £70,000 for his published works, and left an estate of £25,000. When only in his mid-sixties old age seemed to creep upon him prematurely. In November 1882, at age 67, during a happy family gathering, he suffered a stroke, and after lingering for several weeks, died on December 6, just ten years after he had returned from his Australian and New Zealand visit.

INDEX